IMPROVE YOUR YOUR
GOLF

IMPROVE YOUR GOLF

Willow Books
Collins
8 Grafton Street, London W1
1986

Willow Books
William Collins Sons & Co Ltd
London · Glasgow · Sydney · Auckland
Toronto · Johannesburg

First published 1986
©Sackville Design Group Ltd

BRITISH LIBRARY CATALOGUING IN PUBLICATION DATA
Improve your Golf
1. Golf
796.352'3   GV965

ISBN 0-00-218250-5

Designed by Sackville Design Group Ltd
78 Margaret Street, London W1N 7HB
Art director: Al Rockall
Consultant editor: Chris Plumridge
In-house editors: Heather Thomas
Lorraine Jerram
Set in Melior by MacSet Ltd, Wembley
Printed in Belgium by Proost International Book Production

Contents

FOREWORD

Peter Alliss – 'The Voice of Golf'

I am particularly delighted to write the introduction to this book because, although I don't have a great reputation for being a teacher, I have given many golf lessons over the years, particularly in my early days at The Parkstone Golf Club, where I spent thirteen happy years, and at Moor Allerton Golf Club where I was attached for five years.

Latterly, with the television series *Play Golf* and my meetings and conversations with all the great stars, the actual playing of the game and the analysis of the supreme champions have become a fascination to me.

No, I'm not saying that I'm ready to leap up and start teaching beginners. That is one of the most difficult aspects of professional golf and I have the utmost admiration for those professionals, like the ones in this book, who have the ability and the patience to pass on their knowledge in such a gentle way to complete beginners. It can be most frustrating when you meet an enthusiast who has a large enough pocketbook but, sadly, no idea of rhythm, balance or timing. In that case I suppose one must smile politely and take the cash!

My father, Percy Alliss, had a reputation for being a very fine teacher at a time when the teaching of golf was very localized, particularly in the British Isles. Of course, there were always star players and systems in vogue from time to time. In the 1930s, for example, people in Britain talked only of the Bobby Jones or Henry Cotton method. After the war came Ben Hogan, a continuing Henry Cotton followed by Bill Cox, Leslie King and then few others until the stars of the present day.

Of course, it is always much easier to teach good players. The original basic principles are already ingrained so it is more a question of tossing in an idea, or a thought, which can bring an immediate cure in many cases.

In most cases, though, to improve or perfect one's game, hard work and application are needed to supplement basic natural ability. You cannot teach someone rhythm, timing and balance if they do not have a modicum of those ingredients in their body in the first place.

Over the years, *Golf World*, Europe's biggest and best-selling golf magazine, with whom I have had a long and happy relationship, has been blessed with being able to find a superb team of instructors. Well to the fore are John Jacobs, or 'Doctor Golf', who is well known all over the world. His teaching schools throughout the length and breadth of America are now something not to be missed and his reputation there is as great as it is in Britain. Then there is Vivien Saunders, without doubt one of the brightest spirits and most sensible of teachers, not only for women and young people but for all ages, sexes, groups and religions. She really is excellent. Ken Adwick, who was based for many years at Woodlands Manor, and who incidentally taught Neil Coles how to play the game, is another fine instructor, and the team is made up by Ian Connelly, who was the original guide, mentor and tutor to Nick Faldo. The quality of their instruction is matched by the detailed illustrations, the clarity of the diagrams and the ease by which they, and the excellent accompanying photographs, help put the message across in a concise and helpful way.

But remember, there is no magic cure to the problems you may encounter. Everyone who plays the game is striving for the unobtainable. Jack Nicklaus, Tom Watson and Ben Hogan at the peaks of their careers still looked for that magical something. Byron Nelson, when he was playing his best golf, wanted to know how he could improve by just one stroke a round. I know that does not sound much but four strokes at the end of 72 holes? How many times have those great stars finished just one or two strokes behind the winner?

It is the ability to think clearly and eliminate the stupid shots, to manage your golf game, as Jack Nicklaus has so often been quoted as saying. So the top professionals all strive for improvement as well

As a professional golfer Peter Alliss won 20 European tour events. He represented Great Britain 8 times in the Ryder Cup and won the Vardon Trophy twice. He retired from tournament golf in 1969 to embark on a successful broadcasting career, and has become one of the world's most popular television golf commentators

as the beginners. All right, we know it is their business and therefore they have to devote a great deal of time to practice.

That is why I stress there is no magic cure. There are not even any magic ingredients in this book. By just reading it you are not going to suddenly win the club championship. But if you read it, absorb it and make yourself find time to practise and apply a little more thought to your strokes you will be amazed how quickly your game will improve.

This is a beautifully produced book and I know how many people are going to enjoy it. Even if you do not find your handicap tumbling down from 18 to scratch in the space of six months it will make you think and analyze your own game. Golf, you see, is a wonderful game to analyze. It is an endless source of amazement, amusement and discussion. You cannot legislate for genius but it does count for a lot if you get at least half a dozen of the basic principles right before you start. That is what this book will teach you, and it will also help you to refine your game and become a better golfer.

Golf World
'The Leading Authority on Golf'

This book teaches you how to play golf while, at the same time, learning to enjoy the game. It contains the wisdom, practical advice and expert guidance of *Golf World*, Britain and Europe's biggest golf magazine – indeed, Europe's best-selling monthly sports publication. It can help you improve your standard of play and cure faults in your game.

Golf World Magazine is all about excellence and that applies even more so when it comes to choosing the right blend of instruction and the right people to help improve your golf. We believe that we have got the mixture just right. Looking at our team of instructors, whose expertise and wisdom are the basis for this book, John Jacobs has been with *Golf World* since the very first issue back in March 1962, and in the ensuing years he has built up an unparalleled reputation on both sides of the Atlantic. Undoubtedly Europe's best known teacher, back in the 1950s Jacobs was also a world-class tournament player and competed for Britain in the Ryder Cup later going on to captain the team. He is much sought-after as a teacher of national squads and by higher handicap players eager to attend his highly praised golf clinics, and is now recognized throughout the world as one of the top analysts in the game.

Ken Adwick, too, has had a long-standing relationship with *Golf World* and has been a regular contributor to its pages for nearly twenty years. The author of numerous books on the game, his words of wisdom have proved as popular with top pros as they have with complete beginners. His approach to teaching is simple yet thorough and his concept behind the mechanics of the golf swing has stood the test of time.

Scotsman Ian Connelly is yet another expert from *Golf World*'s fine teaching panel and has developed an enormous following in a relatively short space of time. Unquestionably Britain's top teacher of young players, Connelly's sound teaching and advice have been of benefit to players of all ages and standards. Many of the players on the European Tour owe their excellent results to him, none more so perhaps than Nick Faldo who was steered by Connelly from a complete beginner to the ranks of an internationally known sportstar. Connelly's teaching philosophy, which puts great emphasis on the fundamentals of the game, is a proven formula for success.

And finally there is Vivien Saunders whose clear, concise way of teaching has found appreciation from both sexes. A founder member of the WPGA Tour and a former British Ladies Open Champion, Vivien Saunders is also a graduate psychologist which gives her immense knowledge of both the playing and mental side of golf.

Together, John Jacobs, Ken Adwick, Ian Connelly and Vivien Saunders help make up the *Golf World* Professional Teaching Panel, one of the most respected coaching teams in golf. They have all contributed towards making the magazine the authoritative voice in golf today, which is reflected in this beautifully illustrated book.

Golf World is also responsible for organizing the British Club Golfers Championship, and inaugurated the British Isles Long Driving Championship which has given big-hitting amateurs the chance to test their skills against top pros. And from tee right through to green, golfers throughout the land have been able to try their hands in the National Putting Championship run by the magazine.

But perhaps the magazine's biggest sphere of influence is in improving the games of its readers. Through its highly regarded Instruction Schools, members of *Golf World*'s Professional Teaching Panel have literally come to life from the pages of the magazine offering invaluable tuition and the key to making the game more fun. The lessons they teach are to be found in this book which is an essential instruction manual for every golfer – highly readable yet authoritative and packed with expert advice and tips. Read it and you too can play *better* golf!

John Jacobs conducting a golf clinic

Ian Connelly

Vivien Saunders

Chapter 1 THE SET-UP

Good golf starts from a sound foundation. How you set-up to the ball will determine ultimately the direction of your swing, so it is vital to get the foundations of the set-up correct. Yet, many golfers neglect this important aspect and continue to hit unsatisfactory shots as a result. Many of golf's familiar poor shots can be traced back to an incorrect set-up, so it is always worthwhile going back to the basics of the set-up to discover the cause of the fault. This chapter examines the fundamentals of grip, stance, ball position, aim and posture plus information on how to tone up your muscles for golf. Achieving the correct set-up position will require no great physical or athletic ability since it takes place before the club is actually set in motion. Once you have mastered the set-up, then you are well on the way to fulfilling your potential as a golfer.

The key to a good swing

You can only swing the club as well as you set-up to the ball, and if you set-up correctly you are far more likely to play consistently good golf. If you set-up *incorrectly* there is very little possibility of producing the shot you require.

If you watch the top professionals, either during a round or on the practice ground, you will notice the care and attention that they give to their pre-swing preparation. Look at the trouble Jack Nicklaus takes before each shot. He knows how important the set-up is; and all tournament players recognize that if something is wrong with their game then the fault most likely stems from the set-up and not from the actual swing.

In order to reach your full potential at golf, the foundations of grip and set-up must be correct, and developing these foundations requires no degree of skill or athleticism – it is merely a case of care and attention. Let us look therefore at the main factors governing the set-up position.

Posture

The easy way to adopt a correct posture is to stand with your back straight and your weight evenly distributed between your feet. Keeping your back straight, bend over from the waist just sufficiently to give your arms clearance from your body to allow for freedom of swing. Feel that your arms are simply hanging from your shoulders as opposed to being rigid. Flex your knees slightly and place your palms together. Then slide your right hand below the left as it would be positioned on the club.

If you follow the procedure above you will find, as a result of your right side being lower than the left that there is slightly more weight on the right side. You should also feel your weight more towards the balls of your feet.

For long and medium clubs, stand with your feet about shoulder-width apart (measured from the inside of your heels) and gradually narrow your stance for the shorter irons. Avoid extremes: too wide a stance will restrict your shoulder turn and leg action, while too narrow a stance will cause instability. Experiment to find what suits you and if you do happen to err, always make sure that it is on the narrow side.

It is impossible to stand too near the ball provided that your arms have sufficient clearance from your body to allow them to swing both back and through freely. Beware of crouching over the ball and setting your weight on the left side. This position will only encourage 'tilting' instead of turning the shoulders.

Always feel light or 'springy' as you set-up or, as Sam Snead calls it, 'oily'. Light and relaxed muscles will always propel the ball further than will heavy or tense muscles.

Aiming correctly

However good your swing, if you do not aim it correctly it loses most, if not all, of its effectiveness. Logic dictates that if your aim is bad, the only way you can hit the ball at the intended target is by introducing a compensatory error into your swing.

One of the best ways of learning to aim correctly is this: when you are on the practice ground lay two clubs on the ground, one parallel to your stance and the other at right angles to it. The club running parallel to feet and body will help you establish a square set-up, while the club running at right angles will help you to pinpoint the ball position.

It is vital to remember that your

1 An ideal set-up. The head and the upper body are positioned behind the ball

2 The right side is lower and more passive than the left as is shown by the slightly flexed right arm

3 The right knee is cocked towards the target to give the backswing support and stability

4 The ball position is two inches inside the left heel and the left arm and shaft are in line

body line runs to the left of the target, so that if you look directly over your left shoulder you are actually looking to the left of your target. If you look over your left shoulder and see the target directly on that line, then you are probably aiming to the right. This will mean also that your clubhead is aiming in that direction. In the ensuing pages of this section on the set-up, we shall examine in more detail the factors connected with the address position, for it is only by adopting the correct habits at the outset that your game can succeed. If you look like a good player when you stand to the ball, then you have an excellent chance of playing like one.

Relax at address

One of the key factors in the successful execution of a shot is the ability to be relaxed at address. Any tension prior to the stroke will certainly inhibit the free movement of the swing. Tension is something that affects golfers at all levels.

The beginner who becomes tense will often lift the whole rib-cage and produce topped shots. Club golfers tend to tighten their leg and arm muscles in an attempt to exert power, with the result that they achieve exactly the opposite. Top-class players are more likely to tighten up in the hands and wrists with the result that they usually fail to square the clubface at impact; thus producing blocked shots which fall to the right of the target.

The set-up and whole approach to the game is likely to be far more relaxed on the driving range or practice gound than it is in a playing situation. Add to this the burden of playing in a competition and tension can creep in to such a degree that your swing disintegrates.

How to combat tension
Many golfers believe that they must concentrate for every minute of the round. Apart from being impossible, intense concentration of this nature is likely to be destructive – the mind must have an outlet. Lee Trevino is a perfect example of a player who diverts his thoughts while walking towards his ball – but once he arrives at his ball, he switches on the concentration for the shot in hand. Pinpointing your concentration in this manner will help you approach each shot in a more relaxed frame of mind.

Seve Ballesteros demonstrating a relaxed address: the shoulders are dropped, arms hanging loosely, the upper arms close to the body. This position enables the arms to swing easily without power being generated by the shoulders

It is often a good starting point to pinpoint your concentration and relax at the same time, by looking down the fairway at your target and then taking two or three very deep breaths. This simple exercise can help enormously to reduce tension.

Shoulders are the key to relaxation

Tension at address usually emanates from the shoulders. In the correct, and far more relaxed, position, the feeling should be one of standing up with the shoulders relaxed downwards and the arms literally hanging down to take hold of the club. The shoulders should feel as if pushed downwards and the arms should hang relatively close to the sides. If you adopt this position and look in a mirror, the area around the collarbone should appear relaxed, and there should be no sign of tension in the neck or shoulder area.

This position enables the player to swing the arms freely from the shoulders so that arms and body seem to work independently. The golf swing is, in its simplest form, a turn of the body and a lifting of the arms. By relaxing the shoulders, the necessary freedom in the arms can be produced.

The player who is tense at address does not produce this position and, instead, tends to hunch the shoulders up and bring the arms out and forward. Again, a look in the mirror in this position will show the collarbone protruding quite noticeably. From this posture, it is very difficult to swing the arms independently of the shoulders. The shoulders and arms then work too much in unison: the right shoulder exerting power where it is not needed while, at the same time, inhibiting the arms and hands from producing the right amount of clubhead speed.

Golfers at all levels are often unaware of the subtle change in their address position when tension occurs. The key to maintaining a relaxed position at address is to take a couple of deep breaths and then push the shoulders down and back to allow the arms to hang loosely at the side.

Ben Crenshaw at address with a wedge. Note how the ball has been positioned towards the back of the stance

Tall players can make the mistake of crouching over the ball at address which causes tension Nick Faldo shows how a tall player should stand to the ball — no evidence of hunching the shoulders here

Check your grip

The main point to realize about the golf grip is that its chief function is to present the clubface squarely to the ball. The ball will fly straight only if the clubface is square at the moment of impact. This means that the bottom edge of the club – the leading edge – points in the same direction as the line of the swing.

If the clubface is open or facing away to the right of the line of the swing, the ball will slice away to the right. Conversely, if the clubface is closed or facing to the left of the line of the swing, the ball will hook.

Fortunately, the grip that returns the clubface most easily into a square position also helps to produce maximum height and length to the shot. To return the clubface squarely through impact, the feeling should be that the two hands are predominantly to the side of the club. In other words, the left hand is very much to the left of the club and the right hand very much to the right, with the power in the palm of the right hand set towards the target.

The left hand

In adopting the correct grip, the left hand should hang loosely down to the side of the club with the fingertips pointing to the ground. The left hand is then folded over to take hold of the club, with the index finger and thumb kept tightly together. As you do this, there should be a definite line between the left thumb and index

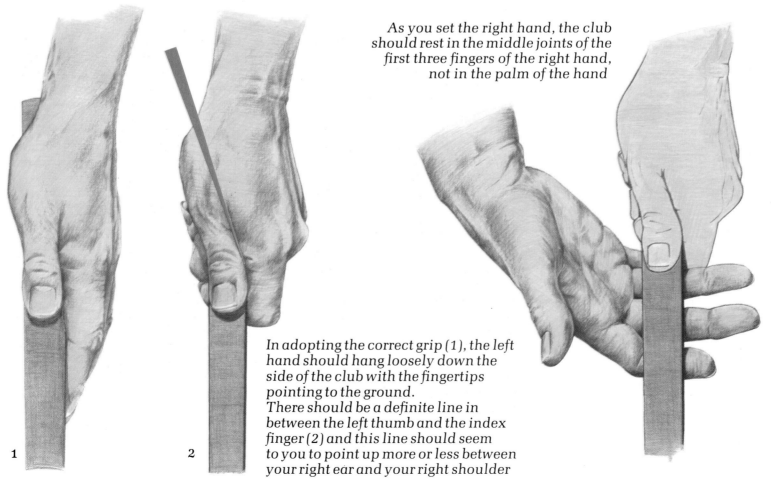

As you set the right hand, the club should rest in the middle joints of the first three fingers of the right hand, not in the palm of the hand

In adopting the correct grip (1), the left hand should hang loosely down the side of the club with the fingertips pointing to the ground.
There should be a definite line in between the left thumb and the index finger (2) and this line should seem to you to point up more or less between your right ear and your right shoulder

1

2

finger, and this line should point up between your right ear and right shoulder. If you then hold the club up in front of you, you should see that the tip of the left thumb and the first joint of the index finger of the left hand are level with one another. The left thumb should not be stretched down the club but should be pulled up reasonably short

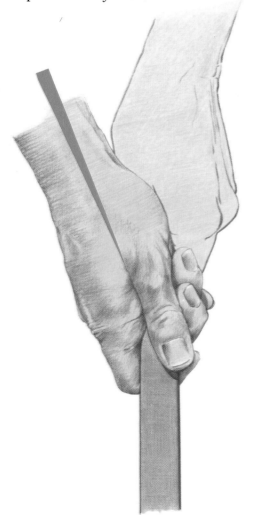

The right hand

As you set the right hand on the club, what you need to feel is that the club is resting very much in the fingers of the right hand. Using the standard Vardon grip with the little finger of the right hand hooked around the index finger of the left hand, the club should rest in the middle joints of the first three fingers of the right hand. The club should not rest in the palm of the hand.

Having rested the club in the middle joints of the three fingers of the right hand, the fold at the base of the right hand is brought into contact with the left thumb. As the grip is completed, the right hand should cover up the left thumb and the left thumb should fit snugly into the palm of the right hand. As you complete the grip, the right thumb should be brought into a position where it is slightly to the left of centre of the club shaft. The right thumb should never point straight down the shaft.

With the right hand in the correct

As you complete the grip, the right thumb should be slightly to the left of centre of the club shaft. It should not point straight down the shaft. The 'V' in between the right thumb and index finger should appear to point up towards your right ear or shoulder

position, you will again see a line or 'V' between the right thumb and index finger. Again, this line should point up between your right ear and right shoulder. The 'V's formed by the thumbs and index fingers of both hands should both point in the same direction, somewhere between the right ear and right shoulder. If you adopt this kind of grip it means that the right hand is very much behind the club, and thus in a position to bring the clubface squarely into impact. If you are having problems with the direction of your shots, it is well worth checking that your grip follows these guidelines. If the right hand is too much under the club with the 'V' of the thumb and index finger pointing *outside* the right shoulder, then the following will happen: as you return the clubface at impact, the right hand will turn the clubface into a closed position and the loft of the club will be reduced dramatically. This will produce a low shot with a hooking flight. If the right hand is too much on top of the grip with the 'V' of the thumb and index finger pointing at the chin or even to the left of it, exactly the opposite happens. This time, as the clubface is returned to impact, the hands will turn the clubface into an open position so that the loft of the club is exaggerated and the clubface aims away to the right: thus producing a high shot to the right.

These then are the main checkpoints; and at the first sign of any directional problems with your game, it is well worth reviewing the grip and checking whether these important lines really are pointing up at the right place.

How to position the ball correctly

In finding the correct ball position at address, it is important to understand how different ball positions affect your swing's angle of attack on the ball. For instance, the further back the ball is positioned in your stance, the steeper your angle of attack; conversely, if you move the ball forward, the shallower that angle becomes until it reaches a stage where the clubhead is travelling parallel to the ground itself.

As a general rule, the younger and better the player, the more hand and leg action is used, so that the angle of attack is likely to be shallower. As a result, the ball is positioned forward in the stance towards the left foot. Older players and the majority of women golfers do not employ so much hand and leg action, so their shallow point will occur earlier in the swing – therefore, the ball should be positioned more centrally.

The first thing to ascertain in establishing the ball position that suits you is to find out where the bottom of your swing occurs. If, for example, the bottom of the swing naturally falls two or three inches inside the left heel, then this should be the standard ball position; or if the bottom of the swing tends to fall directly opposite the middle of the stance, then this should be the standard position from which to work.

Making contact with the ball

Next, you should understand that there are three distinct ways to make contact with the ball: you can strike the ball before the club reaches the bottom of its swing and take a divot beyond the ball; you can strike the ball directly at the bottom of the swing; or, thirdly, you can strike the ball beyond the bottom of the swing so that the clubhead is striking the ball slightly on the upswing.

The first type of contact – the downward contact – is the one you want to use with the short irons, for all types of recovery shots and downhill shots. To encourage this downwards contact, the ball should be played behind the natural bottom of the swing.

For most standard fairway shots, the ball can be struck directly at the bottom of the swing without taking any real divot. This means that the ideal contact is one of nipping the ball off the ground and taking a small divot just after the ball. This is the contact you want from medium and long irons, and also fairway woods when the ball is in a good lie. To play these shots, the ball should be positioned where the natural bottom of your swing should come. For the driver, the ideal contact is to catch the ball several inches beyond the natural bottom of the swing so that the club is travelling on the upswing at impact. To produce this contact, the ball should be played well forward in the

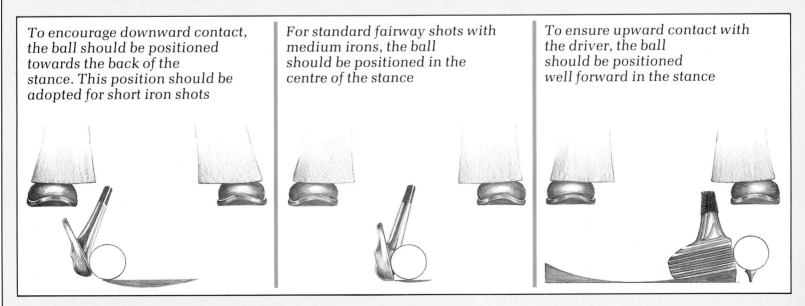

To encourage downward contact, the ball should be positioned towards the back of the stance. This position should be adopted for short iron shots

For standard fairway shots with medium irons, the ball should be positioned in the centre of the stance

To ensure upward contact with the driver, the ball should be positioned well forward in the stance

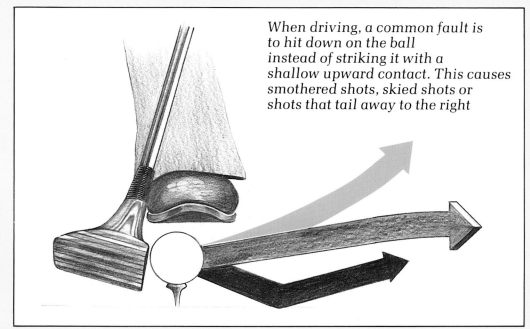

When driving, a common fault is to hit down on the ball instead of striking it with a shallow upward contact. This causes smothered shots, skied shots or shots that tail away to the right

stance, towards the left foot.

One of the most common faults with driving is for the player to position the ball forward in the stance, but instead of bringing the bottom of the swing down eight or ten inches behind the ball and striking the ball with a shallow, upward contact, the player adjusts the swing so that the bottom of the swing now falls at the ball. This is wrong, and produces a downward contact on the ball that causes smothered shots, skied shots or shots that tail away to the right.

Vary the ball position

So there are three basic contacts and these require a different ball position to encourage the right angle of attack. Having decided where the natural bottom of your swing falls, then you can vary your ball position according to which club you are using and what kind of contact you wish to make. When you want upward contact with the driver, play the ball further forward; but when you want downward contact with the short irons from a tight lie, or for recovery shots, play the ball further back to encourage downward contact.

You will notice in altering the ball position that this has an effect on the direction of the shot. When you play the ball further back in your stance, you will tend to strike the ball before the clubhead has reached the straight-through part of the swing. This means that the clubhead will be travelling in an in-to-out path and the ball will fly to the right of target which is known as a 'push'. For this reason, when you are playing short shots or shots from a poor lie and the ball is back in your stance, you have to compensate for the altered swing path by opening the stance and setting the direction of the stance slightly left of target. When you play the ball further forward in the stance for the driver, there is a tendency for the clubhead to strike the ball after it has passed the straight-through part of the swing. This means that the ball could start to the left of the target, perhaps in a slicing flight. To counteract this change of direction, it may be necessary to adopt a slightly closed stance, setting the direction of the stance very slightly right of target. This will bring the direction of the swing on target at the moment of impact.

Adopting the correct position of the ball is fundamental to playing good golf. It is not only important to understand the principles involved; it is also most important to check periodically that you are maintaining the correct position, as it is all too easy to allow the ball to slip back or forward in the stance without even realizing it. Once you get out of position at address, it may change the whole feeling of your swing and throw your game out of tune until the ball position is corrected.

Incorrect positioning of the ball is probably the most frequent cause of loss of form among top players. They constantly check this part of their game and so should you.

Young players tend to use more hand and leg action. As a result, the bottom of the swing is likely to fall further forward in the stance

Aiming along the right lines

Acommon problem for many golfers is one of lining-up correctly. In correctly adopting a 'square' stance, the line across the feet, knees, hips and shoulders should be parallel to the line of the proposed shot. The player is, in effect, standing along a pair of railway lines with the ball setting off down the right-hand line to the target and the body lined up along the left-hand line. However, for many golfers, setting-up in this way is far from natural.

Much of the problem stems from a visual distortion. The player sets-up to the ball and tries to judge a straight line from the ball to the target with two distinct handicaps: first, the player has to judge this straight line without actually having his eyes directly over the line; and, second, he has to judge this straight line by standing sideways to the target. Failing to line-up correctly leads to errors in the swing path.

One of the best ways to overcome any errors in alignment is to stand directly behind the ball-target line. Choose a spot on the ground a few inches from the ball and concentrate on lining-up on this spot rather than on the target in the distance. Having

To line up to the target correctly, imagine that you are playing down a railway track. By correctly adopting a square stance, lines drawn through your feet, knees, hips and shoulders should run parallel to the left-hand rail and parallel to the target whilst the ball should be set off down the right-hand rail directly towards the target

Bernard Hunt shows how practising with clubs laid on the ground can help with alignment

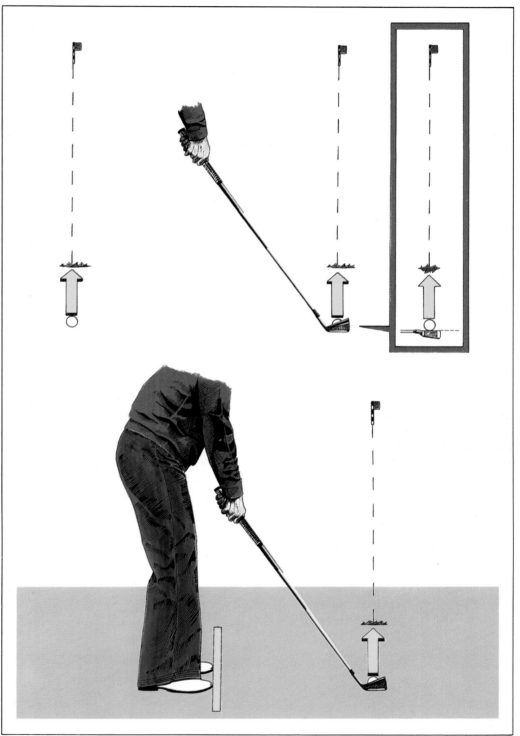

chosen the aiming spot, you should then take up the address position, setting the feet and shoulders parallel to this same imaginary line on the ground. Some players prefer to keep the aiming spot in mind throughout the whole swing, without ever looking at the target until the swing is completed. Other players like to fix on the aiming spot and then look up at the target a couple of times before starting the swing. In doing this, however, there is a danger that the player may feel misaligned and shift around into what *feels* like a more comfortable position. It is far better to pick your spot on the ground, line up on it, and then trust yourself to hit the ball out over it.

To overcome the visual distortion in alignment try this simple routine. Looking from behind the ball, pick a leaf or some other object on the ground some fifteen to thirty inches in front of the ball which is directly in line with the target (top). Then set-up to the ball adopting the railway track routine (bottom). You should now find it easier to check that you are aligned correctly by looking at the object in front of the ball rather than looking at the target in the distance

Loosen-up your golf muscles

In order of priority, the main requirements for playing really good golf are as follows:

1 Temperament,
2 A repeating sound method,
3 Physical fitness and strength.

All of these requirements need to be worked on to achieve consistency and high standards. The efforts we make to achieve a better temperament and method are not always rewarded as we would wish, whereas to be better equipped physically is usually just hard work. The best exercise of all is practice during which time the golf muscles are being used. However, it is particularly in the winter months that efforts can and should be made to get and keep as fit as possible, especially if bad weather stops you playing golf.

To be fit and enjoy the feeling of well-being that comes naturally with fitness is obviously desirable for all activities, but, regarding golf, the hands, wrists, forearms and the legs should receive special attention. If you spend a great deal of time travelling in your car or have a sedentary office job, then keep a squash ball handy and squeeze it whenever you get the chance (not when you are driving, though!). This will help to strengthen your hands and wrists.

The best exercise for strengthening your forearms is to wind up a weight attached to a smooth, circular piece of wood. Tie a strong 90cm/36in length of cord to the weight and then pin it to the piece of wood. Stand with your arms extended straight out in front of you and slowly wind up the weight. This exercise not only strengthens your forearms but aids the wrist and hand action when you come to swing a club.

To strengthen your legs, sit in a chair with your legs stretched out in front of you with weights resting on your ankles. Now, slowly lift and lower your legs. To condition your leg muscles rather than build them up, it is better to lift a heavy weight a few times rather than to lift a light weight a number of times.

The simple exercise of skipping is also obviously beneficial with the added advantage that the lungs and respiratory system also receive attention. Jogging can be aerobically beneficial, too, but is more enjoyable if you have a companion to run with you. Start off slowly and do not attempt too much too soon. Competitive games of squash or badminton are an enjoyable way of maintaining fitness as the competitive element makes it easier to push yourself to the limits of endurance. However, they must be played regularly if you are to receive lasting fitness benefits.

Squeezing a small, soft ball, like a squash ball, at every available opportunity is a good way to strengthen the hands and wrists

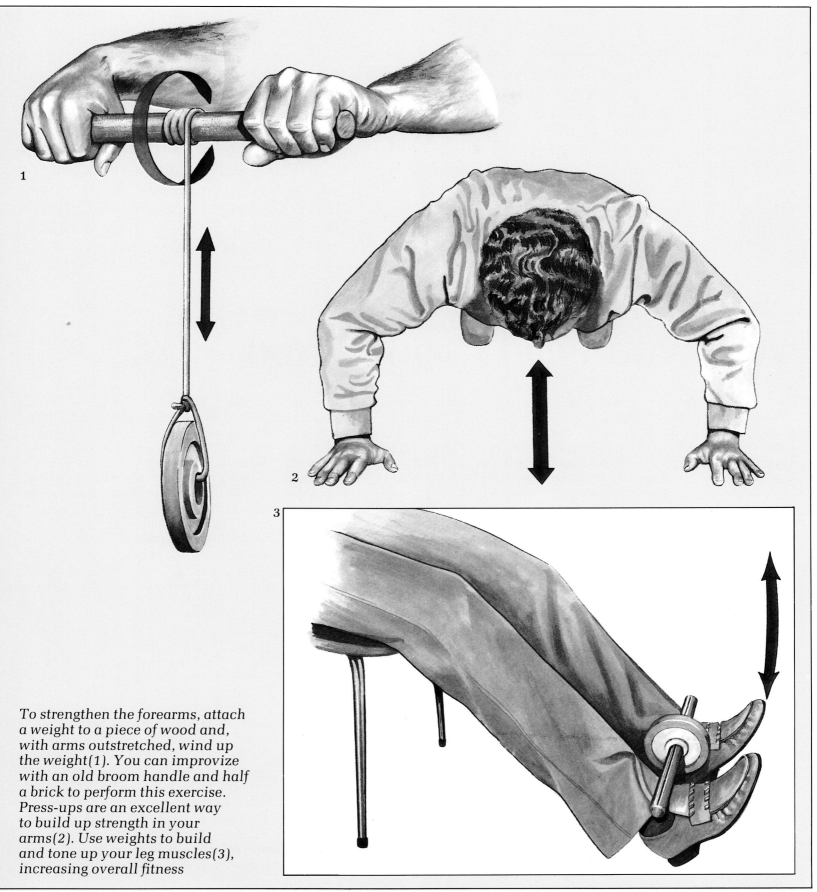

To strengthen the forearms, attach a weight to a piece of wood and, with arms outstretched, wind up the weight(1). You can improvize with an old broom handle and half a brick to perform this exercise. Press-ups are an excellent way to build up strength in your arms(2). Use weights to build and tone up your leg muscles(3), increasing overall fitness

Chapter 2 THE SWING

As the word implies, the swing is a continuous action which allows the golfer to create momentum and speed which can be delivered, via the clubhead, to the ball. The golf swing is not a hit, lunge or a bash – it is a very graceful movement which is designed to create the maximum clubhead speed in a balanced rhythmic manner. In creating this balance and rhythm, the movements of the swing have to be co-ordinated in the correct sequence. This chapter tells you how you can achieve this with the emphasis placed on the tempo of the swing so that these movements have time to take place. A good golf swing, one that consistently delivers the clubhead to the ball square to the line of flight, is founded on a correct set-up and a smooth, flowing action with the minimum of real effort. There is advice on how to hit the ball further, and feet and leg action.

Why you need good tempo

Control is the essence of good golf and your tempo largely determines the measure of control you achieve. The pace of swing at which you can generate clubhead speed under control is the tempo best suited to you. You should swing only as fast or with as much effort as your hands and arms can control the clubhead comfortably.

Effortless power
Most players tend to equate distance with effort, but this is false. Top-class players hit the ball a long way without any apparent effort. This is because all the energy is transmitted to the clubhead, and they know that bodily effort has an adverse effect on the swing.

How many times have you struck a drive miles down the middle and one of your playing companions has remarked, "You didn't seem to put any effort into that one"? The reason your companion made that remark was because it was true! Inevitably, when you step on the next tee, you think that you will apply a little more effort and produce an even better shot and, equally inevitably, you do not. If

anything, you should have swung with even less effort.

Another example would be when you have had to play a long shot to lay up short of a hazard – possibly a lake in front of the green. It is a situation where it does not matter if you are 10 yards short or 20 yards short – maximum distance is not a priority. It is such an easy shot with nothing at stake that all you do is take a smooth, easy swing at the ball only to find that the ball takes off like a rocket and plunges into the water. This is an example of distance being achieved without conscious effort because distance was not the prime thought occupying your mind.

Backswing
The purpose of the backswing is no more and no less than to put the player in a position to make the downswing. Most golfers take the club back (as opposed to swinging it back) too quickly, chiefly because they feel that the faster they go back, the more clubhead speed is generated on the way down. This is a fallacy. An over-fast backswing is usually the result of too much tension at address,

usually caused by anxiety. You should swing the club back with a feeling of lightness in the grip pressure and lightness in the arms. Remember, the pace of the backswing should only be such as will allow maximum control during the change of direction.

Stifle the hit impulse
When a swing breaks down, more often than not it is at the point when the swing direction is changing from going back to coming down. This is caused mainly by an over-fast backswing, but also by an uncontrollable urge to hit at the ball instead of swinging through it. The result is loss of control by the left side and a successful takeover led by the right side. This alters the path of the swing and the position of the clubface to the detriment of the shot. The remedy lies in the words of Bobby Jones: "A golf club should not only be swung back leisurely, it should also be swung down leisurely".

Through impact: the clubhead continues to gradually build up acceleration with the ball merely being in the way as opposed to being hit at.

1

5

2

3

4

6

One of the longest and straightest drivers in the world, Greg Norman creates maximum clubhead speed by maintaining a smooth tempo. An unhurried, one-piece takeaway shows the club shaft as a virtual extension of the left arm(1). As the hands and arms continue to carry the club upwards(2), the left shoulder is beginning to turn to allow Norman to reach a fully coiled position at the top of the swing(3). Just prior to impact(4) and Norman shows that there has been no attempt to hit 'at' the ball as the club is being delivered squarely into the back of the ball. After impact(5) and the clubhead is released freely through the shot and the impetus of the swing carries him on to a full finish(6)

Why you need good tempo

1
2
3

Completion of swing: if the pace of your swing is controlled, you will finish in control of your balance and you should be able to hold your finish indefinitely.

Good tempo does not mean slow
All great players have good tempo but that does not mean that they all swing at the same speed. They develop their own best tempo through an instinctive sense of control and timing.

Compare the tempo of Nick Faldo with that of Tom Watson, for instance. Faldo's most admired swing trait is his smooth, even, slowish tempo. Even when his swing is out of sorts, his tempo has saved him by giving him time to make 'in swing' corrections through a fine sense of touch and feel. On the other hand, Watson has a much quicker tempo, although it looks faster than it actually is. In relation to the rest of his

swing Watson makes a relatively slow backswing, has an easy-paced change of direction and gradually builds up the speed on the downswing. Some players, such as Sam Snead, Ben Crenshaw, Brian Barnes and Sam Torrance, have slow tempos whereas others like Lanny Wadkins and Brian Waites have quick tempos. However, what they all have in common is a tempo that suits them as individuals and is effective in their game.

Gary Player would be regarded as having a quick tempo but it is one that suits him and very few people would argue with his record over the past 25 years. His address position(1) is full of exaggerated good points and from here he achieves a perfect position at the top of the swing(2) with the club shaft pointing at the target. Starting down(3) and already the right leg is beginning to drive towards the ball. Approaching impact(4) and the right arm is hugging the body and then begins to extend as the ball is on its way(5 and 6). The follow-through is poised(7), proof that he has remained in control of the club throughout the stroke

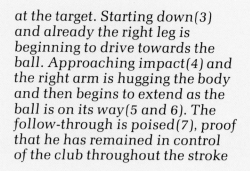

Tempo tips

1 Feel that your pace of swing is the same back and down.
2 Try to swing your driver at the same tempo as you swing your 9-iron.
3 Try hitting a 7-iron about 70 yards with a full swing. You will find that you will hit the ball twice as far because you are in control.
4 Overcoming the hit impulse is a major step towards establishing the pace of swing that is right for you. Swing through the ball, *not* at it.
5 Practise 'swishing' the clubhead. As a 'swish' is created by clubhead speed and it is this that you are looking for at impact, your instinct will discover the best tempo in order to achieve this.
6 Feel light at address and free from undue tension — this will help your tempo enormously.

Swing the clubhead... not yourself

The golf action is called a swing – not a hit, bash or lunge. The very term conjures up such words as 'smooth', 'rhythmic', 'fluent', 'continuous' and 'feel'. This sense of 'feel' should be transmitted to the clubhead as you cannot really swing something without feeling it.

The basic objective in golf is to swing the clubhead forwards in order to propel the ball forwards – good players do just that, whereas not-so-good players tend to swing themselves around and not the clubhead forwards. No matter which method you use, what the ball does is dependent entirely on what you do with the clubhead.

When you look at the great players, you never see a deliberate movement from position to position. Instead,

you will notice a continuous, free-flowing movement back and through the ball. Certainly, positions are important but they must never take priority over free swinging of the hands and arms. The great players swing *through* positions; they do not actually try and achieve them during a swing – there simply is not time to do so.

The swing – a brief description
A brief overall description of the swing would be as follows: stand to the ball free from undue tension, especially in the upper body, gripping the club with lightness and sensitivity in mind. Now swing the clubhead back with the arms in a smooth, unhurried movement, allowing the left shoulder to be pulled to a turn.

Then, in a similar smooth, unhurried fashion, swing the clubhead down and forwards with the arms, allowing the right shoulder to be pulled under and through to the finish. Thus the arms do the swinging and the body responds to the arm swing.

The most fundamental action in golf is the swinging of the clubhead through feel in the hands and motion in the arms. A very good training exercise for this is to stand with your feet close together and hit shots simply by swinging your arms back and through. There is no need to worry about your hips or shoulders or anything else as they will respond automatically. Always bear in mind that swing your arms is a simple concept, and if your concept is simple then your swing will be, too.

The 1985 US Masters champion, Bernhard Langer uses his arms to create maximum leverage and power through the swing. Langer's power stems from an aggressive pulling action of his left arm and leg through the ball. At address(1), Langer starts the club back smoothly and then begins to extend the club away from the ball(2) to create the maximum arc.

At the top of the swing(3) he starts the pulling action down into the ball while his left arm still maintains the width of arc he has created(4). Approaching impact and his upper body still remains behind the ball(5) while his arms continue to swing forward and bring the clubhead into the ball at a position that all golfers should try and emulate(6)

4

5

6

Nick Faldo

Maintaining his wonderfully drowsy rhythm allows Nick Faldo to fully control the club throughout the swing and control of the club means control of the ball. In this picture

sequence, Faldo demonstrates a full swing with an iron which shows how the swinging of the club creates the correct movements in

Bob Charles

Simplicity is the key to Bob Charles' swing and although the tall New Zealander remains the only left-hander to have won the Open

Championship, his swing, if mirrored, would contain all of the good points of a right-handed Open Champion. From address, Charles simply takes

the lower body. For many club golfers it is the other way round. Swinging the club back pulls the left side towards the right leg and

swinging the club down pulls the right side towards the left to provide effort-less power rather than powerless effort

the club back smoothly to the top of the swing allowing the arms to dictate the lower body movements and then brings the club back down again.

There is no attempt to hit 'at' the ball, it is merely in the way of the clubhead and is dispatched with the minimum of effort

Lee Trevino

7

The master of ball flight and control, Lee Trevino's address position(1) reveals that although his feet and hips are open to the target line, his shoulders are square to that line. As he starts the club back(2) the left knee is being pulled inwards(3) as the hands continue upwards. At the top of the swing(4) the legs are poised to provide the powerful drive through the ball(5) and the hands have dropped the club back inside the target line. Just after impact(6) the ball is on its way and on to a typical Trevino finish(7). Trevino is immensely strong, particularly in the legs and this enables him to keep the clubface driving towards the target and create the familiar fading pattern to his shots

Jack Nicklaus

Jack Nicklaus on the practice ground at Augusta National, home of the US Masters, an event Nicklaus has won five times. At address for this short iron shot, Nicklaus lets his arms hang freely down and initiates the swing with that familiar turning of the head to the right. From the top of the swing he drops the club back into the ball, allowing the momentum he has built up to release the clubhead through and on to a balanced finish

Tom Watson

Tom Watson on the practice ground at Royal Birkdale, site of his fifth Open Championship victory in 1983. Watson is extremely strong in the forearms and a very aggressive striker through the ball, using his arms to generate clubhead speed. However, there is no loss of control or balance through this short iron shot as he makes a full turn and delivers the clubhead into the ball with telling effect

THE SWING

Severiano Ballesteros

Since Seve Ballesteros first burst onto the scene in the 1976 Open Championship at the age of 19, his swing has developed into a more controlled action. Points to look for in this sequence are the relaxed address position(1) and the smooth takeaway(2) which enables him to reach a fully coiled position at the top of the swing(3) without any extraneous movement. Approaching impact(4) and Ballesteros has maintained the angle between the left arm and the shaft and is poised to release the clubhead through the ball(5) to a relaxed finish(6)

1

2

3

4

5

6

Sandy Lyle

In this sequence Sandy Lyle, the 1985 Open Champion, demonstrates his mastery of the long irons. At address(1) he is relaxed with the arms extended. The start of the swing(2) shows how quickly he gets the club back inside to the target line as his shoulders, arms and club turn away from the ball in one unit. This puts him in a perfect position halfway back(3) with arms, shoulders and club shaft in a perfect plane. Coming down into the ball(4), note how the clubhead has stayed inside the left arm line. After impact(5), the left side has cleared to make room for the club to swing down the line of the target and back inside the line again to a poised finish(6)

Attack that ball from the inside

Many players have a real misconception about swinging a golf club and striking the ball. Frequently they appear to think that the club should be swung back and through in what approximates to a straight line without in any way swinging it round the body. What should, in fact, happen – certainly with everything from a medium iron to the driver – is that the clubhead must travel in a circular arc away from the ball, up and behind the head, and then attack the ball in a curved arc. If you view the golfer from above and take a line from the target to the ball and out beyond, the club must always attack the ball from inside this line. This is how we get the expressions 'out-to-in' and 'in-to-out'. The clubhead must attack the ball from the inside, strike the ball, and then move on inside again. Correctly, the clubhead should never ever get into the 'outside' area.

What should happen is that the player turns in the backswing, brings the club inside on what may feel to be a fairly sharp turn, and then from the top of the backswing concentrates on attacking the ball in this same curve. What in fact happens with ninety nine per cent of golfers is that the downswing always comes outside the backswing. Frequently players take the club back far too straight and then turn into the shot with their right shoulder and body, thus attacking the ball with an out-to-in swing. This usually results in a straight left pull or a slice away to the right. The majority of players can take the club away exaggeratedly on the inside in the backswing without coming to any

harm. Certainly this is far less likely to cause any error than in taking the club back too straight.

In the backswing the wrists should be hingeing to produce potential power for the downswing. This is not just an upward hingeing on the thumbs. What should happen in the backswing is that the right wrist folds fairly fully back on itself into the position that some professionals describe as being like a waiter carrying a tray above his shoulders. Having reached the top of the backswing the change of direction into the downswing is one of the most crucial parts of the golfing action. The right shoulder is usually in a potentially powerful position and, to most people, it is natural to unwind the right side of the body in an attempt to force strength into the shot. If the right side dominates in this way the club immediately moves into position for an out-to-in, steep attack on the ball.

What should happen is that the left side, which should be dominant in the backswing, remains dominant through the change of direction. The left arm is the key to the change and should pull down or swing away from the right shoulder. Throughout this crucial movement, the right hand should still be cocked back on itself. Again, it is not the hingeing upwards in the wrists that is critical but the folding back of the right hand which determines whether the ball is struck with the clubhead travelling on the right path.

If done correctly and with movements initiated by the left arm, the right hand should still be folded back, perhaps halfway down the down-

swing. The clubhead is then behind the player, when viewed from the player's right side, and is able to attack the ball in the correct curved arc. From this 'late hit position' the right hand is able to generate the maximum possible power by throwing the clubhead out at the ball, through and up to a good finish. This produces an inside and, just as important, shallow attack on the ball.

The player who is able to delay the right hand in this way and to attack the ball with the correctly shaped arc is usually able to draw the ball or hit it straight fairly easily. The shallow attack is ideal for driving and the other long clubs, and maximum distance is obtained.

The correct attack
By contrast, the majority of club golfers approach the ball with far too steep an attack and usually in a straight or out-to-in direction. One of the crucial points in learning to play golf well is to be able to put drawspin on the ball rather than cutspin. The player who has a steep, out-to-in attack will lose yards and yards of distance in both carry and run. The attack on the ball is just like hitting a cut shot at tennis, slicing across the ball and putting on unwanted cutspin. In order to remove his slicing tendency and to encourage draw it is necessary to feel the correct curved attack into the ball.

Left side dominance in the start of the downswing is one thing; another point is simply to feel and concentrate on the path of the clubhead as it attacks the ball. A curved approach into and away from impact produces

a tendency to curve the ball from right to left in the air. Obviously this must go hand-in-hand with a good grip and freedom in the wrists, but as a rule the club golfer attacks the ball in a far more out-to-in direction than ever imagined.

One of the exercises to demonstrate this is to put a light paper cup about fifteen inches behind the ball and an inch or so outside it. The player who attacks the ball in the correct curve should miss this cup every time. But it just does not happen, and frequently low handicapped players who would never imagine that they hit the ball from out-to-in find it virtually impossible to attack the ball from inside the line.

A frustrated slicer?

For the player who has never had the sensation of drawing the ball but is always frustrated with a cutting, slicing action, it is well worth working at starting the downswing with the left arm, feeling that the clubhead is thrown out at the ball in a curve by the right hand, adopting a fairly strong grip, with the 'V's between thumb and index fingers towards the right shoulder and with the hands working loosely and freely through impact. Once the player can sense the feeling of a drawn shot it is usually much easier to correct any unwanted fade or slice.

Frequently the top-class player finds himself or herself falling into a pattern of shots that cut away to the right. Often the curve is virtually imperceptible but the feeling of the shots is weak. The player is often not quite sure whether the ball is being pushed slightly to the right with a little bit of blocking in the hands pro-

Gordon Brand Jnr. shows the way in which the left hand and arms are in control during the change of direction at the top of the swing. With the left arm in control the right wrist is still cocked back, the clubhead being behind the hands and arms approaching impact. This sets the player up to attack the ball from the inside. The right hand and wrist generate power in the impact zone, throwing the clubhead out at the ball with a shallow, curved attack

ducing the cut, or whether he is cutting across the ball very slightly.

Here, again, it is worth experimenting with attacking the ball a little more from the inside, exaggerating the curved attack with the right hand to straighten up the flight.

The essence of a good golf swing

There seem to be two completely different schools of thought as to whether the key to a good golf swing is to concentrate on the backswing or the throughswing. One school of thought says that if you concentrate on the takeaway and get into a perfect position at the top of the backswing, the rest of the swing follows automatically and you cannot fail to produce the correct shot. The other school is that the real essence of a good golf swing is learning to swing correctly through the ball. Obviously both backswing and throughswing are important to a certain extent but those who hold the first opinion almost appear to discount the importance of the throughswing and the follow-through altogether. Their argument is that the backswing controls everything that goes after it. And yet can this really be true? You will frequently see golfers who spend hours and hours on the practice ground trying to perfect a backswing but then hardly make a worthwhile pass at the ball from there. Their throughswing varies from shot to shot so noticeably that the downswing first travels in one path and then in another. The shots are inconsistent and the whole look of the end of the swing tells its own sorry tale.

By contrast, the other school of thought says that the backswing is only the first step to doing the throughswing which is, after all, the part of the swing that hits the ball. If you draw an analogy to tennis, you do

Jack Nicklaus demonstrates the aim of a good backswing with the shaft pointing at the target

The aim of the backswing is to get the club into a position where the shaft is pointing towards the target

The essence of a good golf swing

Work at the idea of swinging the clubhead through the ball in the right direction, at speed. Focus your attention on striking towards the target

not find players of club standard coming in off the court complaining that they could not take their racket back correctly. They do not appear to be over-theoretical and do not become mesmerized by the idea of how the racket should be swung back. All their attentions appear to go on swinging the racket through the ball and striking it on target. By contrast, many golfers are so obsessed by the idea of swinging the club back that they forget about swinging it through the ball, making a good contact and hitting the ball on-target.

The backswing
The aim of the backswing is really to swing the club up into a position where the shaft of the club points on-target – thus controlling the direction of the downswing – while also pro-

ducing sufficient potential energy to swing the club at speed through the ball. For the scratch player and professional golfer, the backswing can become very technical just as it can, presumably, become technical for the tennis player. The club golfer should simply work at producing what is a satisfactory backswing without worrying too much about exact positions. He or she should then work at the idea of swinging the clubhead through the ball in a complete circle with the idea of swinging the clubhead in the right direction, at speed, and producing the desired contact with the ball.

One of the great disadvantages of any method of playing golf that concentrates almost entirely on the importance of the backswing, is that it is very hard to take this method out onto the golf course and to score effectively. You should be thinking of striking the ball on target. If all the concentration in the swing tends to be on taking the club up to the top of the backswing, the mind then has to do a quick about-face to focus attention on striking the ball on target. The player who is obsessed by the backswing can usually perform reasonably well on the practice ground but fails to hit the ball sufficiently consistently on target once he gets onto the golf course. By all means pay attention to the backswing but not to the exclusion of swinging the club correctly through the ball.

Think of the backswing as being purely preparatory to swinging the club through the ball and keep your swing very much target-orientated once you get out onto the golf course.

Many top players concentrate on swinging through to a very definite, well-balanced, follow-through position. This maintains tempo and keeps the swing going in the right direction

The action of the feet and legs

Golf is a game where it is necessary to co-ordinate the correct movements of the arms and legs. For the club golfer, the arm action is often mastered reasonably well but the leg action tends to be ignored. If the foot and leg action is ignored, there is always the tendency to produce a forcing kind of action with the upper body and shoulders. The player who slices the ball is often guilty of having poor leg action. This means that he or she has to bring the shoulders into play excessively in order to produce any sort of power at all. So let us have a look at the correct movements in the feet and legs.

In the set-up the weight should be concentrated slightly on the insides of the feet so that the stance is approximately hip or shoulder width. In this way the knees should be knocked in very slightly, which means that they will usually move correctly through the rest of the swing. The weight is concentrated slightly on the balls of the feet and not back on the heels if anything. As the backswing takes place the weight in the left foot moves from being flat on the foot forward onto the ball of the foot. To compensate for this, the weight in the right foot moves back towards the right heel. As this weight transference takes place, the left foot may need to bend slightly so that the left heel comes off the ground.

Certainly the pressure should be taken off the left heel even if the left heel does not appear to come right up off the ground. For most golfers the weight transference in the backswing usually does not cause real problems. However, what can cause a problem is when a golfer is under the misconception that the weight should roll on to the very inside of the left foot. This is quite incorrect. If you set the feet

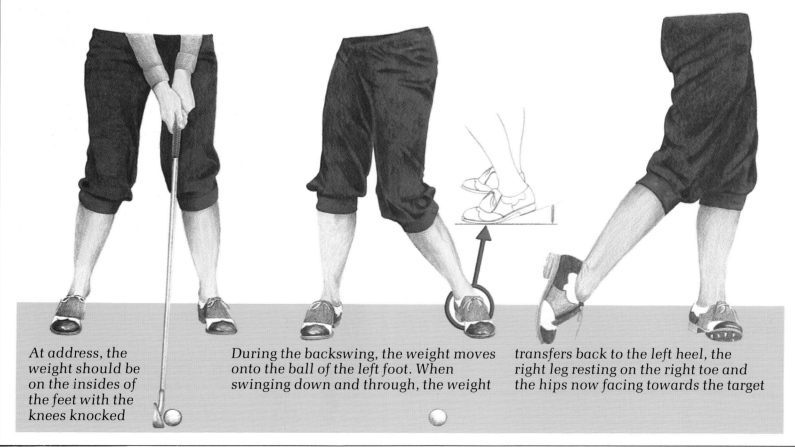

At address, the weight should be on the insides of the feet with the knees knocked

During the backswing, the weight moves onto the ball of the left foot. When swinging down and through, the weight

transfers back to the left heel, the right leg resting on the right toe and the hips now facing towards the target

The fluid leg action of Tom Watson ensures that the upper body stays behind the ball as the club begins its downward path

in what is exactly the right address position, a movement forward onto the ball of the left foot will mean that the left knee will point in somewhere behind the ball. This will take place automatically unless you set yourself up incorrectly at address with the knees pointing slightly outwards instead of having them knocked slightly inwards. Provided that the set-up is correct, all you need to feel is that the weight in the left foot moves slightly forward as the backswing takes place.

How to stop swaying

If you get the wrong weight transference in the backswing and the weight is allowed to move onto the inside of the foot so that there is a kind of rolling action, this, in turn, will mean that you are almost certain to sway towards the ball as the downswing takes place. So remember that the movement is very much a forwards and backwards movement and not a question of merely rolling the foot on to the inside.

Having got up to the top of the back-swing, which usually causes relative-ly few problems, most golfers are somewhat inhibited in using their feet and legs sufficiently freely in the downswing. What should happen in the downswing is this: the first move-ment should be to push the weight backwards onto the left heel. If the left heel has been allowed to rise in the backswing it should be pushed firm-ly back down onto the ground. The heel should then stay flat on the ground right through the remainder of the swing.

Having pushed the left heel firmly back to the ground to start the down-swing, the right leg and right foot must be allowed to move freely. The right foot should spin through onto the tips of the toes so that by the end of the swing the sole of the right shoe very definitely faces out behind the player. If the right foot is allowed to

At the top of the backswing the left heel will probably come off the ground slightly (far left). Moving the left foot out wider at address may help to produce more freedom in the throughswing without restricting the backswing (left)

The action of the feet and legs

move freely in this way it will also mean that the right knee and right hip turn on through to the target. Many golfers try to produce what is a mistaken feeling and that is one of twisting the *hips* through to the target. On the whole, you will find that most golfers who try to spin the hips through tend to produce too much turning with the rest of the upper body and usually find that the shoulders come into play too much. If, on the other hand, you think largely of spinning on through with the right foot this automatically means that the hips get into the correct position. For most golfers it is usually far simpler to think of the right foot and the correct action in this than to produce the right sort of movement by concentrating on the hips. The lesson to be learnt is that if you get the foot action correct the hip action will fall into place.

Therefore, what you should see in the throughswing is the left heel being pushed back onto the ground, the weight moving backwards into the left heel and the left knee becoming firm through impact. This is combined with freedom in the right leg and right foot so that the right side of the body spins on through until the weight is concentrated on the tips of the toes of the right foot. There is, however, one other area of the leg action that tends to be slightly difficult and therefore often ignored by the club golfer. In the address position the left foot should be turned out very slightly. Then as the down and throughswing takes place the hips should turn on through so that they finish facing the target itself.

This produces the overall direction of the golf swing. What this means is that by the end of the swing the left foot is still pointing more or less in the same direction while the hips have turned on through. This means that there must be a very noticeable twist in the left leg during the throughswing to enable the foot to point in one direction while the hips face in another. For many golfers who take up golf as adults, this twisting movement can be something of a problem and is often the real reason why the leg action tends to be too static and the resulting swing is flat-footed.

Getting the action right

There are two remedies for the problem outlined above. First of all, it is most important to find the best position for the left foot at address. Theoretically you could turn the left foot out to point in the direction in which you propose to hit the ball. This would help encourage the correct type of throughswing and it would take away the necessity to produce this slightly difficult twisting in the left leg. Turning the left foot out excessively in this way would, however, produce a very restricted backswing. It would mean that almost certainly the player would have difficulty in producing a sufficient turn of the shoulders to set the club on target at the top of the backswing. If, on the other hand, the left foot points straight out ahead of the player at the address position this produces plenty of freedom in the backswing but tends to be very restrictive for the throughswing. Any

player who has difficulty in producing the correct sort of movement through the ball, should therefore experiment to a certain extent with the left foot position to find the happy medium between allowing freedom in the backswing and freedom in the throughswing. It may well be that by turning the left foot out very slightly more at address the player suffers no restriction in the backswing yet produces rather more freedom in the throughswing. The second remedy is simply one of practising the leg action of the throughswing over and over again until the left leg happily twists itself into the correct position where the hips can face on target.

With the leg action working sufficiently freely the end of the golf swing should see the weight concentrated very much on the left heel and the tips of the toes of the right foot. There should never be any feeling that the weight in the left foot at the end of the swing is at all concentrated on the ball of the foot or towards the toes. There should certainly never be the feeling of having to curl up the toes of the left foot in order to struggle to maintain balance. Correctly, the weight transference in the left foot should be one of moving forward onto the ball of the foot and then pulling the weight backwards onto the heel of the foot as the downswing and the throughswing take place. For the player with an inhibited foot action, a couple of hours' practice on the driving range wearing track shoes or tennis shoes, which allow the feet to bend freely and encourage the right type of active movement, is an excellent idea.

At address(1) Curtis Strange's knees are flexed and as he starts the backswing(2) the left knee is pulled in towards the right(3). At the top of the swing(4) and the right leg has remained firm but still flexed ready to push off as he starts the downswing(5). Approaching impact(6) and the knees are sliding through towards the target with the right leg providing the drive(7) that carries him on to a balanced finish with the weight on the outside of the left foot(8)

The route to lower scores is provided by greater control of the golf ball. This control can only be attained by correct striking. Knowing why the ball exhibits different characteristics in flight is a major step in improving your control of it. It is also important to know how the loft on each club can affect the flight and control of the ball and to translate this into distance and accuracy. This chapter gives you a clear insight into these factors and provides you with a greater understanding of what happens when the clubface strikes the ball. Learn also how to use your fairway woods.

Contact and what it means to your game

The vast majority of club golfers appear to assume that every bad shot in golf is caused by a faulty technique or bad swing. However, this is simply not true. It is possible to play very good golf and to score consistently with an unorthodox swing. What you must remember is that the whole purpose of any golf shot — whether long game or short game — is to hit the ball from A to B. The factor that controls whether the ball travels on target is the contact you make with the ball. The purpose of the golf swing, therefore, is to contact the ball correctly. What the club golfer often fails to realize is that it is perfectly possible to produce an orthodox swing and yet make a poor contact with the ball; conversely it is possible to produce an unorthodox-looking swing and yet strike the ball perfectly. If the club golfer hits a bad shot, he or she will almost always assume that there must have been something wrong with the swing.

There are really three different kinds of contacts that one has to produce with the ball. The first contact used with the driver is to strike the ball slightly on the upswing. With the long irons and fairway woods, you attempt to strike the ball at the very bottom of the swing, just nipping the little piece of ground on which it sits.

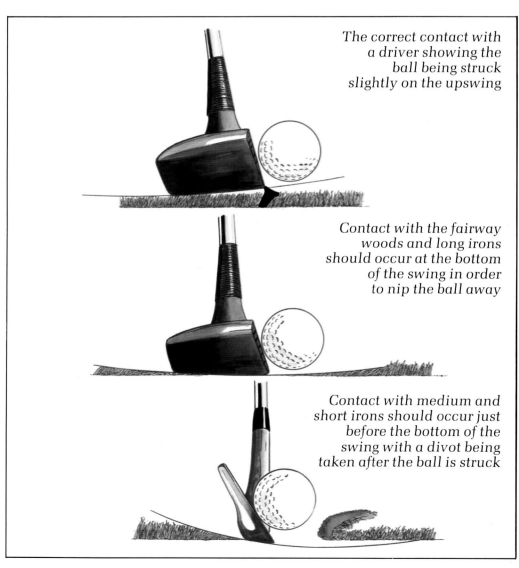

The correct contact with a driver showing the ball being struck slightly on the upswing

Contact with the fairway woods and long irons should occur at the bottom of the swing in order to nip the ball away

Contact with medium and short irons should occur just before the bottom of the swing with a divot being taken after the ball is struck

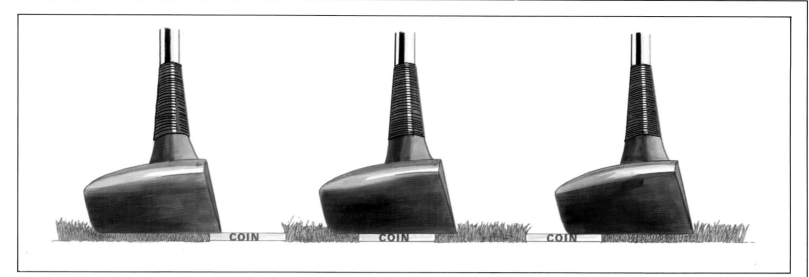

On the other hand, when you use a medium or short iron, or in any recovery shot, the ideal contact is to strike the ball on the downswing taking a divot beyond it. What you are also aiming at doing is to catch the ball from the very centre of the club. Particularly with the second type of contact (the one used with the fairway woods and long irons) the aim of the swing should be to brush the little piece of ground on which the ball sits – this target being no larger than the size of a very small coin. Obviously, if you think about it, it takes a great deal of co-ordination and a very well trained eye to be able to swing the clubhead from address right up to the top of the backswing and then down again and to brush this spot perfectly accurately. The clubhead does, after all, have to travel through an arc of, perhaps, twelve feet before returning to brush the ground at this spot.

Often, the club golfer is able to produce a reasonably good-looking swing which gives the impression that he or she should be able to play good golf. However, what this player fails to realize is that the accuracy at contact simply is not good enough. Instead of brushing the ground in a small area the size of a small coin, the medium-handicap player probably brushes the ground anywhere within an area an inch to an inch-and-a-half in diameter. If he is half an inch out one way he will be catching the ball

With fairway woods and long irons the clubhead should brush the small area of ground on which the ball sits. This target should be no more than a very small coin (above centre). Most medium to high-handicap players do not have this accuracy. Half an inch either side of this imaginary coin (above right and left) can ruin a good-looking swing by the ball being caught slightly heavy or slightly thin

very slightly heavy: if he is half an inch out the other way the ball may be slightly thinned. Swing down fractionally too close to the feet and the ball will be caught slightly from the toe of the club; swing out too far and you have a potential socket. In looking at the higher handicap golfer, you frequently find that his area of contact with the ground is anything up to three or four inches. He simply has not got the accuracy to strike the ball consistently. The swing may repeat itself reasonably well but being that inch or so out at contact spells disaster. Whereas one shot may be heavy, the next may be thin. In fact, the depth of contact may be entirely wrong so that he or she digs right under one shot or completely tops the next. However, what you must realize is that this is not necessarily through bad technique.

Much of the problem for the medium- and long-handicap golfer is that he or she fails to realize just how

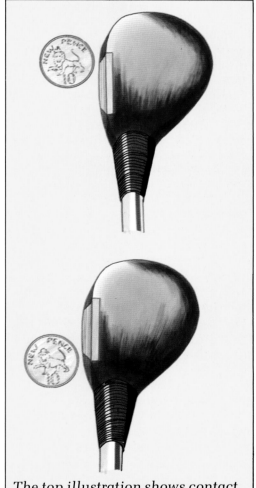

The top illustration shows contact with the toe of the club caused by swinging down too close to the feet. The bottom illustration shows contact with the heel of the club caused by swinging out too far

Contact and what it means to your game

important the contact is. There seems to be an assumption that providing you swing the club in the orthodox-looking manner the ball should go correctly. There is often total lack of awareness of the importance of striking the ball or indeed the little piece of ground beneath it with accuracy. Very often the club golfer goes for a lesson and the pro will say, "Have a couple of practice swings". The pupil does three or four perfect-looking practice swings and then says to the professional, "There, you see I can do it without the ball". The professional, however, is not so convinced. He has probably been looking at the contact the player has made with the ground and will have quite possibly seen four practice swings which all brush the ground in completely different places. Whether any would have struck the ball correctly is doubtful.

In learning to play golf, a high proportion of golfers are quite able to produce a really good-looking swing after just a couple of lessons. However, because the ball is so small and there is also the added problem that it sits on the ground, the first attempts at striking the ball are usually disastrous. The accuracy of contact simply is not good enough — unless the player is blessed with excellent ball sense and perfect co-ordination. The player sees these first dismal efforts and instead of simply working with the swing he has learnt, so producing better and better contact with the ball, he tends to fiddle around with the swing and assumes that the swing must be technically very difficult. By contrast, the child learning to play golf will usually stick to his

Club golfers should learn a simple, basic swing. They should keep in mind the idea that the swing is aimed at moving the clubhead to the top of the backswing and swinging it through a circle, brushing the ground at the exact spot where the ball lies

The professional golfer focuses on the ball and his whole mind is concentrated on making the right contact

natural swing and go on swinging away at the ball until he achieves the accuracy he wants. For him the game is comparatively simple. The adult, on the other hand, is usually convinced that his or her initial failure with the game is because of lack of mastery of the technique of the swing. This, to a certain extent, is a fallacy. Obviously, to play top-class golf the swing is technical; no doubt to play top-class tennis the various strokes involved are equally technical. Whereas the club tennis player will usually be relatively unconcerned with his technique, the club golfer is often obsessed by it. The best suggestion for the club golfer is that he or she learns a simple, basic swing, keeping central in the mind the idea that the whole swing is aimed at moving the clubhead up to the top of the backswing and from there swishing it through in a circle, brushing the ground at the exact spot where the ball lies. Having learnt this basic swing, you should practise developing accuracy of contact. The best exercise is simply to have repeated practice swings concentrating on making the clubhead brush the ground at the exact spot you wish. If you cannot do this in the practice swing you are unlikely to be able to do it with the ball.

For the professional golfer, almost all the thought in the long game, apart from perhaps one piece of technique, is in striking the ball correctly. The professional has his eyes focused on the ball and his whole mind is concentrated on producing the right contact. The club golfer by contrast often tends to ignore this. If you tend to catch the ball fractionally thin, concentrate your whole mind on brushing the little piece of grass on which the ball sits. If, on the other hand, you talk to yourself hard enough you will go a long way towards producing what you want.

Do you need a driving lesson?

The old golfing cliché is that you 'drive for show and putt for dough'. However, for the club golfer the drive is probably the most important part of the game. Any club golfer who can manage to drive the ball consistently and hit the fairway with reasonable length from every tee is usually well on the way to producing a good score. But for most medium-handicap golfers who may have few problems in producing the required distance, it is often an odd bad drive here or there that can ruin the good score. Even with virtually top-class amateurs and also professionals, an erratic drive is often the difference between winning and losing.

Choosing your target
One of the main keys to driving the ball well is to have the right mental approach to the shot. It is absolutely no good expecting to hit the ball right down the centre of the fairway unless you can make yourself think really positively about the shot that faces you. First of all, it is absolutely vital to choose a definite target at which to aim. It is no good simply standing on the tee and trying to hit the ball somewhere down the fairway. What you must do is to pinpoint a target – either a tree in the distance, the flag or a bunker or, if there is nothing definite on the horizon, try to *imagine* a target on the fairway. Many golfers fail to choose an exact target and then wonder why they do not hit the ball down the middle. For this reason it is

This impact position shows why Greg Norman is one of the longest, straightest drivers in the world

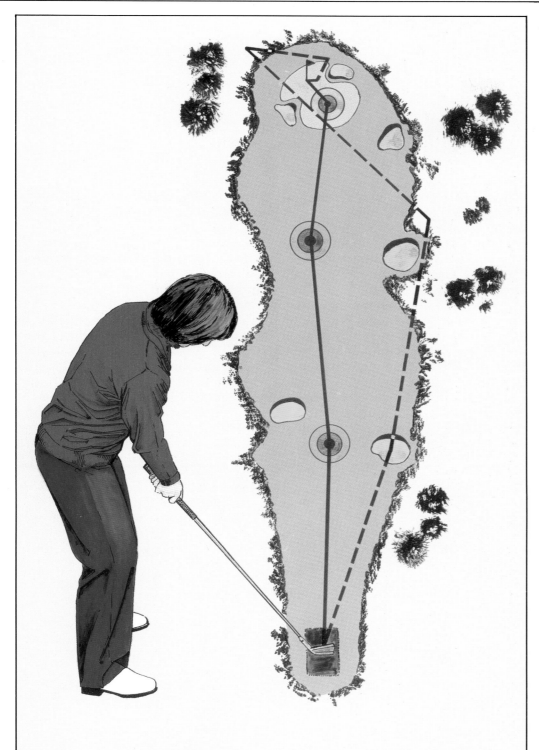

One of the keys to driving the ball well is to think positively about the shot you are going to play. Choose a really definite target at which to aim and concentrate on this. If there is nothing obvious on the horizon, then try to imagine a target on the fairway. Remember not to think of places you do not want to go. If you think negatively and focus your mind on the hazards, you will probably end up in them!

often almost easier to drive the ball well on a really tight golf course because your mind then tends to be attuned to thinking of a definite target all the time. If you are faced with a wide open course with seemingly few trees or other obstacles, it is often all too easy to become sloppy about choosing a target and to find driving becoming more and more erratic.

Having chosen the target you are aiming at, it is then essential to think of this and this alone. What many golfers do is to think of the places they do *not* want to go. If you stand on a tee and your mind is focused on the bunkers on the left, for example, with the idea of *not* hooking the ball into these, this mental picture may become so strong that it acts as a form of instruction and you produce just the hook you did not want. The thought must never ever be negative in this way. So do the best you can to block out any thoughts of where you do not want to go, and if you find yourself standing over the ball with the wrong kind of negative picture in your mind, walk away from the ball and then start all over again. This is hard to do, but if you hit the shot with the wrong mental picture a disaster is inevitable and you will probably kick yourself afterwards for not starting all over again.

Positioning yourself

Having decided upon the exact place to which you are trying to hit the ball, it is most important to set yourself on the correct side of the tee. If you tee up the ball on the right-hand side and then aim towards the centre of the fairway, you will be turned automatically towards the left of the hole. If, on the other hand, you tee the ball up on

Do you need a driving lesson?

the left of the tee you will be facing automatically slightly more across the fairway towards the right. You will frequently find that you can get a completely different view of a hole by teeing up on one side or the other. Professional tournament players are usually very careful about where they tee the ball. You will see them walking the width of the fairway to discover the position that produces the best look to the drive. On the other hand, the club golfer and, indeed, many top-class amateur golfers tend to follow one another like a flock of sheep teeing up in exactly the same place as the previous player.

If you are trying to position the ball down the left of the fairway or if most of the trouble is on the right of the hole, you should be teeing up as far over to the right of the tee as possible. This will mean that you are helped automatically in aiming to the left. Conversely, if all the trouble is down the left of the hole you should tee up as far to the left as possible so that you are hitting automatically away from this. Do spend time over this preliminary. Five seconds' extra thought can make life considerably easier. Added to this, you should be looking for a suitably flat place to tee the ball or a slightly upward slope. All too

often, club golfers tee up the ball in the last place the professional would choose.

The importance of a practice swing
So, having chosen a positive target and teed up the ball on the correct side of the tee, what is the next rule? It is a good idea to have a practice swing before every drive. This acts as your kind of dress rehearsal to set your swing into the right groove. As you do this, look at a spot on the ground where the ball would be in relation to your feet but then ensure that the bottom of the practice swing is nice and shallow and falls several inches

If the trouble on a hole is down the left, tee the ball to the left side of the teeing ground. This will give you the feeling of playing away from the trouble

behind where the ball would be. This encourages the correct upward contact. Work at a full practice swing and do this at much the same speed as your swing with the ball will be. If you slow the whole swing down too much, the nature of the movements involved can be altered. So invest in a full dress rehearsal and imagine the ball flying off just as you would wish.

Striking the ball

Now, the really important part – striking the ball. What you must appreciate with the drive is that it is absolutely no use hitting it half-heartedly. Obviously the swing should be sufficiently controlled to be perfectly balanced at the end of the follow-through which may give the impression that you are swinging within yourself. However, the player who drives the ball well hits it hard with a confident, free-flowing swing. Whatever you do, do not try to steer the ball. Having chosen your target, make as good a swing as possible and swing hard on through to a balanced follow-through. Any tendency to try to steer the ball down the fairway instead of to swing at it will mean almost certainly that the swing slows up by impact. If your tendency is to slice the ball, then slowing up will probably mean that you will leave the clubface open; if your tendency is to hook, slowing up gives the wrists too much time to roll over and the clubface will tend to close. So, choose your target and have sufficient courage to swing the clubhead fast and freely through the ball into a perfectly balanced follow-through. If anyone tells you that you are trying to hit the ball too

hard, this almost certainly means that you have come off balance.

Finally, it is often amazing what a little extra willpower will do! Try going out on the golf course and keeping a really strict record of just how many fairways you do manage to hit from the tee. If in your next round of golf you only hit eight fairways, set yourself a target of hitting at least nine on the next occasion. Assuming that there are four par threes on a course you should be able to work your way up gradually until you can hit thirteen or fourteen fairways in the round. For most golfers a little extra concentration or even a small wager on the side will often work wonders!

Knowing your distance can lower your scores

There is no doubt that good driving and well-hit shots to the green go a long way towards setting up a good score. There are two important factors in hitting second shots which set you up for birdies and pars. The first, of course, is that you have to hit the ball straight. The second is that you have to hit the ball the correct distance.

What is vital to appreciate is that 10 yards left or right of the flag is equal to 10 yards short or 10 yards past the flag. Although this sounds obvious, the majority of golfers either fail to realize this or, even if they do, they do not improve accordingly. The good golfer who pulls a ball with a long iron 10 yards left of the flag is quite likely to be disgusted with himself. On the other hand, he is also likely to leave the shot 10 yards short or even 20 yards short and hardly realize his error. The point is this: if you hit the ball out to the side of the target, the error shows. If you hit the ball short of the flag (or, unusually, past the flag), the error is usually not apparent. A shot 10 yards to the side of the flag will look bad. A straight shot 10 yards short will probably look extremely good. And yet there is still 10 yards error, creating just the same problems in making the birdie or the par.

In playing pitch shots, exactly the same is true. Hit the ball a few yards left or right with a medium-length pitch and it looks a disaster. Leave it six or seven yards short and it looks good or almost perfect – looks good, that is, until you walk up close and the hidden ground starts revealing itself.

Judging distance well is an essential part of good golf. For the low-handicap golfer there is usually a 10-yard gap between adjacent clubs. Given that most greens are somewhere between 20 and 40 yards in length, it is obvious that with bad clubbing one can be two, three or, into the wind, even four clubs out and still be on the green. The error is almost always one of being short.

Most people do not naturally judge distance as well as they probably think they do. On flat ground with no real distance cues, you will probably find it well nigh impossible to judge distance accurately. If you go out on the practice ground or into a park, pick out a spot, try to assess the distance in your mind and then pace off the distance to see just how accurate you are. Most people can be 30 or 40 yards out in judging a distance of 150 yards or so. Obviously when you are out on the golf course you have certain things that help you with judging

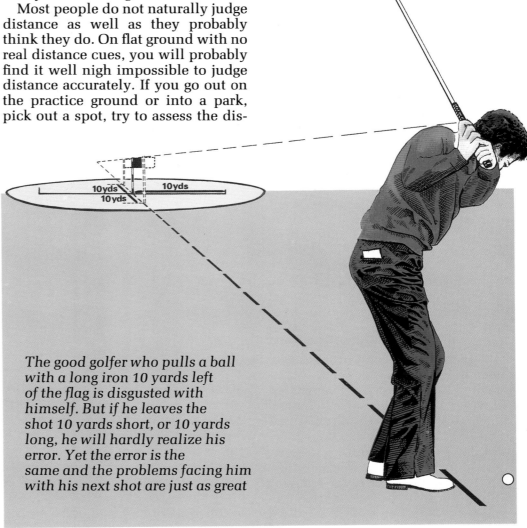

The good golfer who pulls a ball with a long iron 10 yards left of the flag is disgusted with himself. But if he leaves the shot 10 yards short, or 10 yards long, he will hardly realize his error. Yet the error is the same and the problems facing him with his next shot are just as great

To help you attack the flag on an unfamiliar course, you should know the distance to the front and back of each green and also to any problem behind the green. In this way, you can be far more positive in choosing the longer of two clubs because you know your club selection is quite safe

your distance. The players in front will act as some kind of distance cue; so too do the flag, bunkers and trees. You may also learn from experience on your own golf course the distance involved. But although most golfers of a relatively low handicap imagine that they can judge distance fairly accurately by eye, their judgment is probably nowhere near as accurate as they imagine.

To judge a distance of 150 yards as opposed to 160 yards, purely visually, is virtually impossible. Once you are six or seven yards out with your judgment you are also probably a club out in your selection. For this reason, almost all top professionals and amateurs pace off distances round the course in order to give themselves absolutely accurate information in club selection. Judging distance is just as difficult, if not more so, than judging time or speed. And yet most of us rely on a wrist watch for telling the time or a speedometer in a car for assessing speed. Do not be fooled and assume that you – unlike Jack Nicklaus or Tom Watson – can judge distance perfectly by eye alone! Almost certainly you cannot!

Many golf courses now have well prepared yardage charts available in the pro's shop which are a tremendous boon for both visitors and members alike. If you are an aspiring player then it is well worth using the distances accurately. Simply pick out a landmark on each hole, the back of a bunker, a certain tree or whatever, make a note of this and then pace the distances to the front, middle or back of the green as you prefer. When you first use this technique you may well

find it extremely difficult to forget what your eyes tell you and to rely almost entirely on the distance involved. Obviously in those wretched dry, bouncy conditions we face in the summer months, judgment has to be a little more subjective and you have to be prepared for an unpredictable 50 or 60 yards of bounce. But on well-watered courses, and height of the summer apart, having accurate information as to the distance involved soon encourages attacking club selection and more positive striking.

Ability to attack
One way to develop the ability to attack the flag well on a course with which you are relatively unfamiliar is to ensure you know the distance to the front of each green, the back of

each green, and also to any problem area behind the green. In this way, you can say to yourself, "Ah yes, I've got 180 yards to the flag, 195 to the back of the green and 210 before I hit trouble". Thus, you can be far more positive in choosing the longer of two clubs while knowing your selection is quite safe.

The club golfer, of course, may not wish to be involved with all the paraphernalia of a little notebook and distances, pacing around and holding up everyone behind. But then again, even on his own course, knowing the distances is a tremendous help. You do not have to measure all the distances on one occasion; gradually pick out odd trees or other very clear landmarks, pace off your distance to the middle of the green and either retain the information mentally or jot it down on a card. You will find this added knowledge useful over and over again and it will soon teach you just how far you hit each club.

Know the laws of ball flight

Successful golf is a result of ball control rather than 'swings' of which there have been many successful, but very different, ones. If we accept this basic concept regarding ball control, then what the clubhead is doing when it hits the ball is the determining factor above all else. The key factors at impact are: clubhead speed, clubface alignment, the swing path and the actual angle of approach to the ball.

Ideally, we would like an impact with maximum clubhead speed with the clubface square and the swing path on line with the club reaching the ball at the appropriate angle of attack. When this is not the case, the ball itself is the best indicator as to what has gone wrong. However, when all is said and done, the ball can start only left or right of the desired line which indicates the swing path. It can curve only left or right in the air, which indicates clubface alignment relative to the swing path. Ball trajectory gives a clear indication of the angle of approach of the club to the ball – a shallow arc through the ball will fly it relatively low whereas a steep, narrow arc tends to fly the ball much higher.

If a player sets-up with an open stance, this leads to a steep angle of approach and a high trajectory shot(1). The trajectory and flight of the ball are the best indicators of the position of the clubface at impact. A ball flying left has been hit with a closed face(2); a straight shot means a square clubface at impact(3) and a shot to the right shows the clubface was open at impact(4)

One of the difficulties of playing golf is that many players are often not achieving what they think they are doing. A simple illustration of this is when the ball finishes to the left and most golfers assume that they have hit out-to-in. However, a quick look at the divot may show that the swing path was straight or even to the right of target. This confirms that the ball has gone to the left because of a closed clubface. In fact, the clubface is quite the most important factor of the impact dimension since if this one is wrong, the swing path and, therefore, the angle of approach of the club to

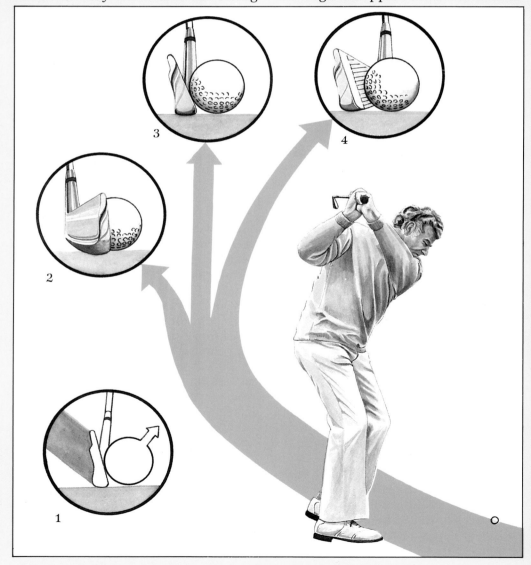

It is important to understand how the loft of the club affects the spin on the ball. The straight-faced clubs, which make contact near the centre of the back of the ball, impart side-spin (right). Lofted clubs hit the bottom of the ball, which causes backspin rather than side-spin (far right), even when the clubface is open

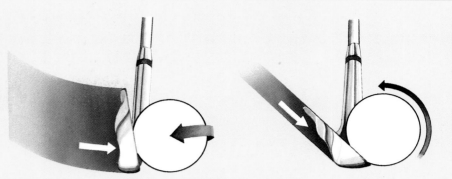

the ball will quickly follow suit.

If the clubface is making contact with the ball in an open position, the vast majority of players will automatically swing out-to-in. This leads to a too-steep angle of approach of the club since fear of going to the right will dominate. Conversely, if the clubface is closed at impact the swing path will automatically become in-to-out which actually leads to the bottom of the arc being behind the ball and thus an upward blow being delivered.

The out-to-in, open clubface, steep angle of attack will work reasonably well with the pitching clubs but not with the straight-faced ones. The closed clubface and in-to-out upward attack very often drives the ball quite well if sufficient loft is used on the club, but the pitching clubs will suffer since the necessary ball-turf contact is unobtainable.

One further aspect that needs to be mentioned and understood is how the loft on the club affects the spin applied to the ball. It is only relatively straight-faced clubs, which make contact near the centre of the back of the ball, that can impart side-spin. Therefore, the straight-faced clubs give the best indication of the club-face position at impact. The lofted clubs obviously strike the bottom of the golf ball and, therefore, impart backspin as opposed to side-spin, even when the clubface is open.

It follows, therefore, that an out-to-in impact with the clubface open will create a left to right slice with the straight-faced clubs, such as a driver or long iron, but will tend to pull shots straight to the left with the pitching clubs since, in this instance, backspin will be predominant. This explains why so many golfers slice their long shots and pull the short ones. It is important to make an effort to understand your own ball flight in terms of the impact since this understanding is the real step to lasting improvement in your game.

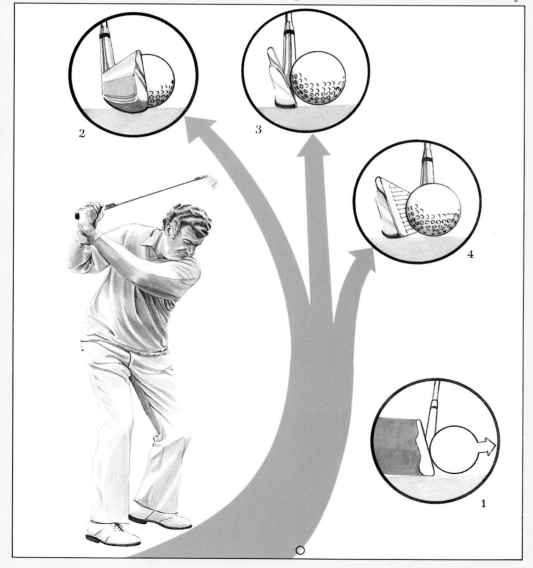

A closed stance produces a relatively shallow angle of approach and a low trajectory shot(1). As before, the flight of the ball will tell you how the clubface was at impact

How you should use your fairway woods

The first point to appreciate in playing the fairway woods is that the standard wood shot requires a special kind of contact. With the iron shots, on any kind of bare or less than lush lie, you are usually trying to nip the ball away with some kind of divot just beyond the ball. With fairway woods the contact is different. The sole of the club should brush smoothly along the ground at the moment of impact, judging the depth of contact to a fraction of an inch in order to get the whole ball on to the clubface and into the air. All too often, good iron players who strike the ball with a slightly descending blow, play their fairway woods in the same way, often with unsatisfactory results.

Whenever the whole of the ball, or virtually the whole of the ball, is above ground level, the takeaway should be wide and low. This encourages a sweeping contact so that the clubhead just grazes the ground at a perfect depth. To achieve this, the ball should be played somewhere just inside the left heel – or wherever the bottom of your swing naturally falls – with the right arm and right shoulder hanging below the left and without the hands pushed unduly forwards. Let the arms hang naturally.

A wide, shallow takeaway

Now concentrate on a wide, shallow takeaway but also ensure that the clubhead goes back on its natural curve and is not forced straight away from the ball. Remember, a slightly curved takeaway will usually be a shallow one; a takeaway that forces the club straight back becomes steep and chopping.

Having swung the club away in a shallow curve, give yourself time to reach the top of the backswing without forcing the distance. Concentrate on watching the ball well through impact and try to produce a shallow, skimming contact en route to a full, balanced follow through.

Resist any idea of beating down into the ball as you might with an iron. Instead, try to perfect your depth of contact so that you could hit one shot after another from exactly the same spot on the ground, leaving the ground unmarked and yet catching all of the ball. For those players who

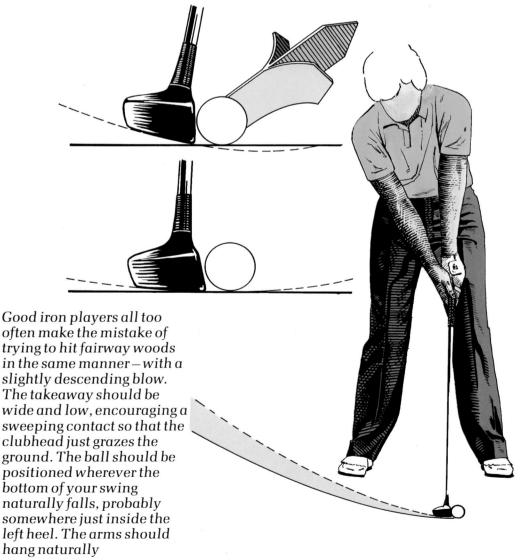

Good iron players all too often make the mistake of trying to hit fairway woods in the same manner – with a slightly descending blow. The takeaway should be wide and low, encouraging a sweeping contact so that the clubhead just grazes the ground. The ball should be positioned wherever the bottom of your swing naturally falls, probably somewhere just inside the left heel. The arms should hang naturally

find problems in feeling the depth of contact in this way, do not be fooled into imagining that a fairway wood with a huge head is going to improve your chances. A neat, compact head is far more likely to put weight beneath the middle of the ball and send it soaring away.

Most poor wooden club players have some element of an unsatisfactory, descending blow into the ball, smothering shots and without any consistency of strike. Work at a clean, smooth contact as though sweeping the ball off a sheet of glass. Once the depth of contact is perfected, it is possible to move down to a 2-wood or even a driver off the fairway with little fear about producing good flight and accuracy. Obviously, the fluffier the lie the easier these long woods become but the principle is the same.

Occasionally we are faced with semi-recovery shots with a shorter

wood. Many players realize the wisdom of using a 5- or 6-wood from a miserable lie in the rough or fairway. If the whole of the ball is not above ground level, sitting in a slight depression or divot, the fairway wood can still be often much easier to use than a long iron. A chunky-headed little wood will often fit into a bad lie

When using a fairway wood the best contact to achieve is as though you were sweeping the ball off a sheet of glass. Match your thoughts for a shallow attack on the ball with an equally shallow, curved takeaway

How you should use your fairway woods

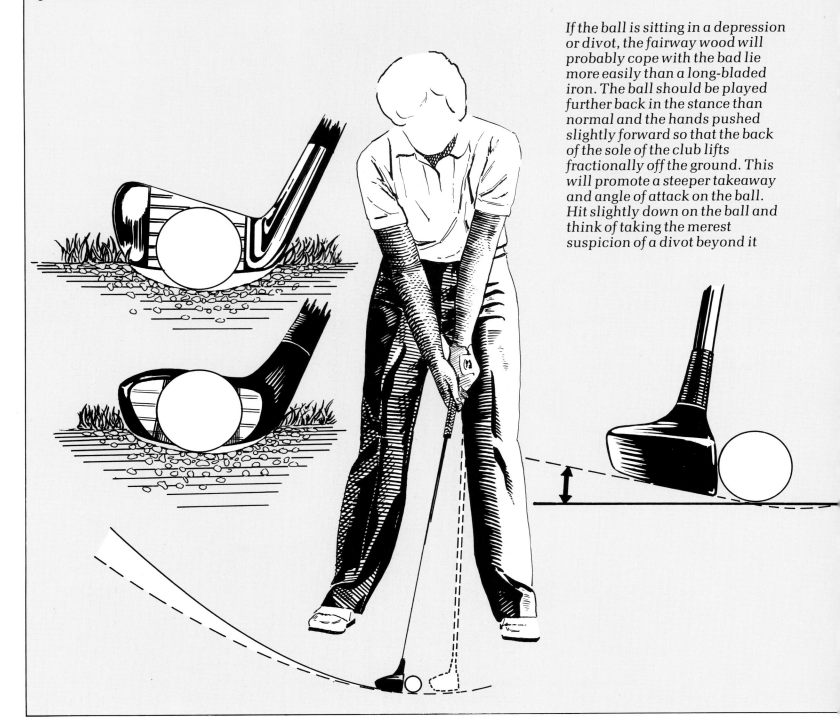

If the ball is sitting in a depression or divot, the fairway wood will probably cope with the bad lie more easily than a long-bladed iron. The ball should be played further back in the stance than normal and the hands pushed slightly forward so that the back of the sole of the club lifts fractionally off the ground. This will promote a steeper takeaway and angle of attack on the ball. Hit slightly down on the ball and think of taking the merest suspicion of a divot beyond it

more readily than a long-bladed iron. From a poorish lie, the ball is now played further back in the stance, around the middle of the feet; the hands are pushed slightly forwards to encourage a more downward attack, and in this way the back of the sole of the club lifts fractionally off the ground. The swing now becomes more like a medium iron, the take-away being allowed to be a little steeper, though still on the inside, and the thoughts of the contact focusing on hitting slightly down through the ball with the merest suspicion of a divot just beyond it. As a rule this kind of contact is marginally less accurate than the perfect, sweeping contact from a reasonable lie.

Good fairway wood play requires development of the perfect depth judgment, skimming the ground and not chopping into it. The fairway woods are, in many ways, so much easier to hit and control than the long irons, allowing bold, attacking shots which fly into the heart of the green.

Johnny Miller (top) in a classic position with a fairway wood, note how his head remains over the ball. Bernard Hunt (right) plays a fairway wood from a poor lie: for this shot the ball should be positioned further back in the stance. David Graham (far right) shows how the club is kept on line through the ball

Chapter 4 THE SHORT GAME

No matter how good your long game is, there will be occasions when you have to rely on your short game to save par. Remember that a delicately executed chip or a long putt holed counts as much as a booming drive. Since a golfer uses the short irons more than the clubs designed for longer hitting, it stands to reason that the more accomplished you are with these clubs, the lower your scores will be. Furthermore, par allows you to take two putts on every green so the putter is by far the most used club in the bag. In this chapter you can learn how to execute those stroke-saving short shots, how to recover from bunkers and how to hole more putts. By adapting these techniques into your game, you can quickly lower your scores and thus improve your game.

Three stages to perfect chipping

For many golfers the ordinary little chip shot from around the green is often made unnecessarily difficult. Part of the problem is frequently in choosing the wrong club. You should play these little shots with the 5-, 6- or 7-iron. Longer handicap golfers are often tempted to use an 8, 9, or wedge from around the green which makes life much too difficult. The long-handicap player should start with a 6-iron. The reason is this: if you play the shots with one of the medium irons in this way the length of the swing required will be very much the same length as a swing with a putter from the same distance. If, therefore, you should be unfortunate enough to thin the ball you will probably find that it goes very much the right distance. If you use one of the more lofted clubs, the length of the swing will have to be rather longer. Should you then have a poor contact with the ball it is likely to go much too far and scuttle through the green. So, the medium irons give more room for a little error.

The first stage in chipping is the one that applies to the relative newcomer to the game. For him, the idea of the chip should be that it is very much like a putt but with a lofted club. The first problem is to teach the player to get the ball airborne every single time but without thinning it through the green. The drawback for most long-handicap players is that they have an urge to try to lift the ball by flicking it upwards with the hands and wrists. All this does is to make the clubhead catch the ball somewhere around its middle and push it straight out along the ground. What you have to do is brush the little piece of ground on which the ball sits so that the loft of the club can do its work and produce the right kind of height.

The first stage should, therefore, be to adopt a rather stiff, wooden position at address, holding the club well down the shaft to give greater control. The feet should now be fairly close together, with the weight well onto the left foot. This will help to resist any tendency to fall backwards and attempt to scoop the ball. At address, the left arm should be extremely firm with the left wrist absolutely locked. What you need to produce is a little swing with the clubhead moving back and forwards through a relatively short arc. The clubhead should be kept very low to the ground, the legs being allowed to move freely but with the chief idea in the mind being to keep the left wrist very solid through impact. The incorrect action of the long-handicap golfer usually sees the left hand and arm stopping just before the moment of impact with the right wrist flicking the club on through. The ideal practice technique to produce a basic chipping action is to practise swinging the club back and through with the left arm only. The main aim of this first stage is to produce a solid contact, brushing the ground on which the ball sits.

Once you have mastered this first stage satisfactorily and, therefore, can be certain that the ball will get airborne, the next stage is to try to produce rather better feel for distance and direction. The basic idea with all chip shots is that the longer the shot required, then the further back and through the club should be swung – backswing and throughswing being of identical lengths.

The second stage is aimed at producing rather greater sensitivity. This is done by relaxing the legs a little more and also by relaxing the arms so that the elbows may now be allowed to bend noticeably. This should relieve a certain degree of tension and make the hands and fingers rather more sensitive. The shot is then played in very much the same way as the first stage, stressing the firmness in the left hand and wrist and also ensuring that the left arm is

Tom Watson (left) shows why firmness through the shot is vital for successful chipping. The relaxed position of Severiano Ballesteros (above) is the key to his mastery of the shorter shots

kept moving through impact. Any tendency to stop the left arm will again produce the incorrect wrist action which can be so disastrous. In this stage it is also very important to ensure that the legs begin to work freely, with the right knee coming on through towards the target as you strike the ball. In order to produce accuracy with chip shots you will also find it helpful to open the stance: by turning your feet towards the left of target. The shoulders should, however, be kept reasonably square. By turning the body in this way, it means that one can become rather more target orientated and really very much like the position you would adopt in throwing a ball to a target. You would probably instinctively face diagonally towards such a target. Just the same applies in chipping. For the player who is now trying to develop

Three stages to perfect chipping

rather better feel, the ball should be played much nearer towards the toe of the club than for ordinary full shots. In the long game your aim is to hit the ball solidly and as far as possible. Striking the ball from the centre of the clubface should help you produce maximum distance. However, in the short game, your idea is to produce really perfect feel so that you have absolute control of the ball. You will usually find that if you play the ball closer towards the toe of the club that this part is much more sensitive and it may help you to get the ball much closer to the hole.

The second stage of chipping is the one for the majority of golfers right down to those in the single figure handicap range. Once you get down to single figures, your idea now should be that you want to hole the ball with every chip shot. Your sights should now be much higher, and what you want to do is to develop perfect feel. By this stage you should not have any difficulty with the actual contact you produce with a ball so that there should not be any danger of either thinning the ball or hitting it at all heavy. To produce the best possible touch around the green, play the shots with the hands, wrists and fingers. To produce maximum feel in this way the whole body should be very relaxed – the stance opened towards the target – ball addressed towards the toe of the club and the eyes firmly focused on the back of the ball. The really good golfer is then able to play a neat little chip shot almost entirely with the hands and wrists, just concentrating on nipping the little piece of ground on which the ball sits and almost striking the ball slightly on the upswing. This is the method that you will see the majority of professionals using but is most definitely not the one to be copied by all but the good golfer.

So, learn your chipping in these three definite stages and do not try to run before you can walk by adopting the method the professionals use when you simply are not ready for it. The first priority is a sound contact with a firm left wrist; the second stage allows you to relax slightly and also encourages better feel; the third stage is the one for the top-class golfer and once mastered will enable you to get close to the flag on every occasion.

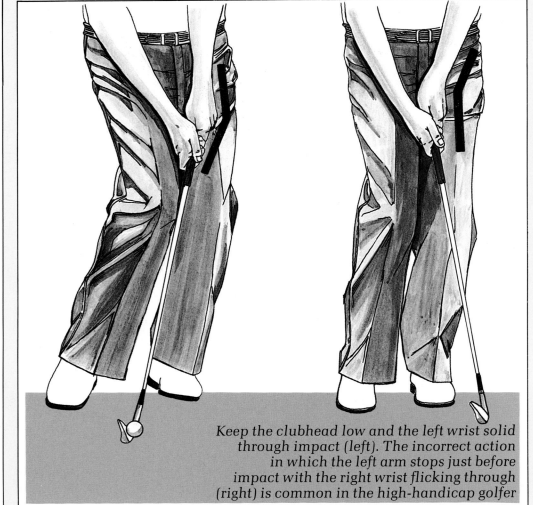

Keep the clubhead low and the left wrist solid through impact (left). The incorrect action in which the left arm stops just before impact with the right wrist flicking through (right) is common in the high-handicap golfer

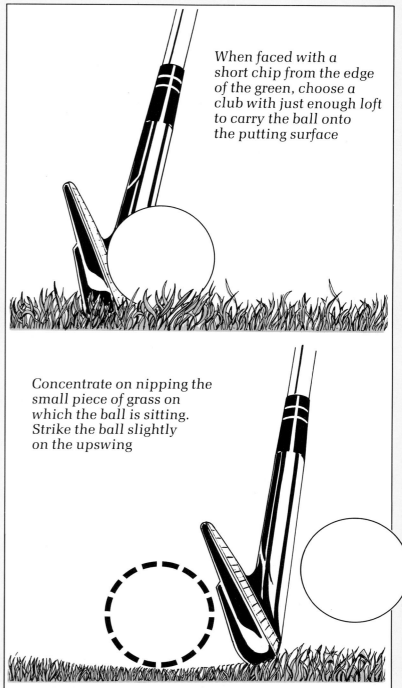

When faced with a short chip from the edge of the green, choose a club with just enough loft to carry the ball onto the putting surface

Concentrate on nipping the small piece of grass on which the ball is sitting. Strike the ball slightly on the upswing

To set-up correctly, adopt an open stance keeping the shoulders reasonably square. Your eyes should be firmly focused on the back of the ball. Address the ball towards the toe of the club

The up and over pitch

One of the shots that is most intimidating to the longer-handicap player is the little pitch over a bunker onto the green. This becomes even more intimidating when the flag is very close to the bunker or when the ground from which you are playing is rather bare. In learning to play this little pitch, you should note that the name 'pitching' is applied not only to this kind of short shot but also to shots of perhaps up to 100 yards for a single figure player. You may read articles that describe a method of pitching that is entirely different from this one. If so, the writer in question is probably thinking in terms of a much longer shot.

When you are playing a little pitch of this kind, it is most important to select the correct club. Club golfers frequently attempt to play this shot with a 9-iron or even an 8-iron. The professional golfer, on the other hand, will almost always use a sand wedge. Think of it this way: if you use a 9-iron it means that you are going to produce a lower shot with considerably more run. In order to stop the ball close to the hole, you will have to pitch the ball a very short distance over the bunker. In many circumstances, a perfectly played 9-iron simply would not pull the ball up quickly enough. If, on the other hand, you select the sand wedge, it means that you are going to produce a higher shot which has far less run. There-

fore, with this club you are able to pitch the ball further over the bunker, leaving yourself more room for slight errors. Club golfers often think that the sand wedge is purely and simply a club to use in the bunkers – this is a fallacy. The sand wedge, being the most lofted club in the set, can be useful for all kinds of recovery shots and particularly for this kind of pitch. The only kind of sand wedge that is really unsuitable for using for pitching is the one with an exceptionally large flange where the leading edge of the club sits well off the ground. Women golfers are often afraid of a sand wedge because it is so heavy and, if hit incorrectly, the shot goes off with too much speed. However, it

You should have the feeling that you move the legs to make the arms move. If you use no leg action, the swing will then come from the shoulders which will create tension

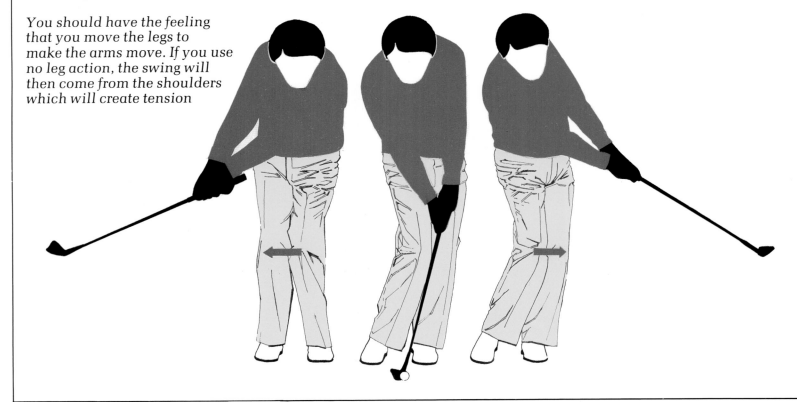

Sliding the blade of the club under the ball has enabled Bernhard Langer to execute a soft-landing recovery shot from heavy rough

is silly to be afraid of the club; learn to play it well and it can be the most trusty weapon in your bag.

What you require to play this little pitch shot is a kind of pendulum action, swinging the club back and through by using the arms and legs and cutting out all wrist action. This will produce a safe shot which will not let you down even under pressure.

In address, position the ball almost opposite the centre of the stance, with the shaft of the club coming straight up towards you and the hands a few inches down the grip. The weight should be set slightly on the left foot, opening the stance a fraction towards the left of the target and adopting a wooden arm position so that there is no question of the wrists crumpling during the swing.

In order to execute the shot, you want to feel that the left wrist stays perfectly firm throughout the backswing and throughswing so that the arms swing as a unit. The end of the club will start at address close into your body. It should never be allowed to move very far away from you so that the arms are not allowed to stretch away to the side, but the whole swing is kept neat and compact. In order to play this shot perfectly, the feeling should be that you move the legs to make the arms move. You will find that if you simply allow the legs to turn a little to the right this will virtually force your arms back so that the whole body and arms stay in one piece. This is completely different from leaving the feet firmly planted on the ground and allowing the legs to become static and inactive.

The up and over pitch

If you use insufficient leg action the whole swing will then come from the shoulders, thus creating tension and producing an awkward-looking swing with very little feel. So make the movement of the legs move the arms and keep the end of the club fairly close into the body.

As you swing through the ball, the weight should be transferred very firmly onto the left foot so that there is no question of trying to scoop the ball into the air. At the moment of impact it is essential to watch the ball really well and to concentrate on brushing the ground beneath it. Again, the legs are kept moving on through while you must think also of keeping the left arm moving. If the left arm is allowed to stop the wrists will fold up and the club will come off line. So, again, it is a question of using the legs to make the arms move and keeping the end of the club shaft fairly close into the body. In this way, the whole swing is executed by a smoothly coordinated movement of legs and arms, without using any wrist break. The length of the shot is simply controlled by the length of the swing – keeping the backswing and throughswing identical lengths so that the halves of the swing mirror each other.

In executing the shot on the golf course, there are two very important points. First of all, of course, you have to produce the correct contact. To do this, have two or three practice swings, concentrating above all on clipping the ground with the bottom of the clubhead. Swing the club back and through and brush the ground. This is finding your depth of swing.

The second point is to make the ball travel the correct distance. The first element of this is to choose a spot on which the ball should land, allowing for the right amount of run. Having made your choice, the next task is to make the ball land on this spot. After your two or three practice swings to find the desired depth of swing, the next stage is to look at your target and to produce a clear picture of it in your mind. You should then be able to focus your eyes on the back of the ball and yet retain a perfect picture of your imaginary target. With this in mind, visualize the shot you are trying to produce and concentrate simply on swinging smoothly back and through and brushing the ground beneath the ball. As with all other shots in golf, it is useless having a negative image of

Keep your left wrist firm throughout the action and keep the left arm moving through. If you stop the left arm, the wrists will fold and the club will go off line

what you do *not* want. If you imagine the ball trickling into the bunker in front of you, then this is what is going to happen. The picture in your mind *must* be positive as this is the set of instructions on which your brain is going to work.

The shot does become more difficult as the lie becomes slightly bare but it should be approached in exactly the same way. If there is an inch of soft grass under the ball, there is clearly far more room for error on your part through impact. When the lie is bare you simply have to judge the depth perfectly. However, there is no need to approach the shot in a different way. It just needs confidence and steady nerves. By restricting any wrist action and producing this kind of pendulum swing, you should develop a short pitch shot that will stand up to all kinds of pressure. Only when the bottom of the ball is sitting slightly below the level of the ground do you need to use a wristy action, picking the club up in the backswing and nipping the ball out with a divot. Tournament golfers will sometimes use this kind of pitch even from a good lie, but as soon as any wrist action is adopted there is more chance of the shot going dreadfully wrong. So play these up and over pitches with the sand wedge, using a reliable, no-wrist pendulum type of action if you want success.

Choose a spot on which the ball should land, allowing for the right amount of run. Look at the target and produce a clear mental picture of this when you look back to the ball. Always think positively

The long pitch can add bite to your game

In learning to play the pitch shot properly it is essential to realize that there are two distinct shots. One is the little shot used to play over a bunker just around the green and the other is the longer pitch shot of up to 100 yards which is simply an approach shot into the green. We feature the second of these two shots. It is important to appreciate that this is *not* the shot to use when faced with a small, delicate shot round the green.

The long pitch shot can be played with the 9-iron, pitching wedge or sand wedge. The decision is a question of the length and height required. A lot of professional golfers use a sand iron in preference to the pitching wedge in order to produce more stop on the ball as it lands.

In setting up to the ball, you should play it well back in the feet, that is well towards the right foot. Having the ball back in this way encourages you to strike it on the downswing, taking first the ball and then a divot beyond it. With the ball well back in the stance the hands are now ahead of the ball. The weight is concentrated on the left foot and from this position you should feel able to attack the ball very much on the downswing.

What makes the long pitch a rather unusual shot in golf is that the two halves of the swing do not mirror each other as they do in most shots. In the majority of golf shots, backswing and throughswing should be of virtually identical length. If you produce a full backswing you should produce a full throughswing and if, as in the chip shot, you use a short, controlled backswing the throughswing should be equally short. This is not the case in the long pitch. The wrists break early and freely in the backswing while the throughswing is short and punchy, so that the two halves of the swing are entirely different.

In the backswing, the hands should have the feeling of working early and freely so that the club is picked up with a rather narrow, upright backswing. The weight should still be mainly on the left foot with the left arm – as in all shots – firmly in control

Bernhard Langer shows the importance of the left arm driving through into a firm, controlled position beyond impact

of the club.

From the top of the backswing, the feeling must be one of producing a firm, downward attack on the ball, striking it and then taking a divot beyond it. For the longer-handicap player, there must be no tendency to fall back onto the right foot in an attempt to scoop the ball up into the air. The feeling should be one of driving hard onto the left side, producing a descending attack on the ball which squeezes it up into the air. By playing the ball back in the feet and having the hands ahead of the ball at address, this downward contact should be fairly easy to produce.

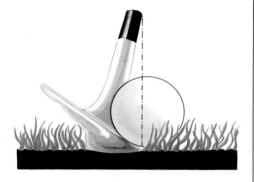

Any tendency to 'scoop' the ball into the air will close the clubface prior to impact and result in hitting the ground behind the ball (right). Concentrate on hitting down into the back of the ball and let the loft of the club propel the ball upwards (far right)

What is so important in the long pitch is that the left arm drives through into a firm, controlled position beyond impact. The left arm does not fold away into the body as it does with the full shots with an iron or a wood. Instead, the finish of the swing should be no more than waist height with the eyes still focused on the spot on the ground where the ball was originally. The left arm is firm and extended and the right foot is through onto the tips of the toes to allow the arms freedom to get into this position.

The actual execution of the shot should not be particularly difficult but what is tricky is to be accurate with the shot in terms of both distance and direction. The essential with this shot, as with all others, is to get the ball from A to B. With the long game the technique of the swing may require hours of practice to perfect, but with the short game the hours of practice are needed to produce sensi-

Set-up to the shot with the ball well towards your right foot, most weight on your left foot and your hands ahead of the ball. This allows you to attack the ball first and take a divot second

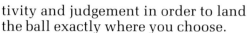

tivity and judgement in order to land the ball exactly where you choose.

Direction of the long pitch

As far as the direction is concerned, many players find it very difficult to hold the correct line with a long pitch. Whenever the ball is played further back in the stance encouraging the downward contact, there is also a tendency to strike the ball on an in-to-out direction. In other words, the ball is being met slightly earlier in the swing than usual so that the clubhead has not come through onto its on-target path and the line of the swing is aimed to the right of the target. To compensate for this, the line of the feet should always be opened very slightly – that is, turned fractionally to the left, so that the club travels on target as it strikes the ball. The golden rule with any recovery or semi-recovery shot is to play the ball back and open the stance.

For the person who invariably pushes the ball to the right with pitches, the simple answer is to adjust the line of the stance. But you often find players who have had instruction or read articles suggesting that the line of the stance should be opened, and they either open the stance exaggeratedly thus pulling the ball to the left, or they adopt an open stance without having the ball sufficiently far back. For the person who pulls the ball, the solution will be in the ball position and line of the feet.

For many low-handicap golfers the problem with direction is often not a question of a consistent push or a consistent pull. Instead, the shots often simply lack accuracy and the ball is

The long pitch can add bite to your game

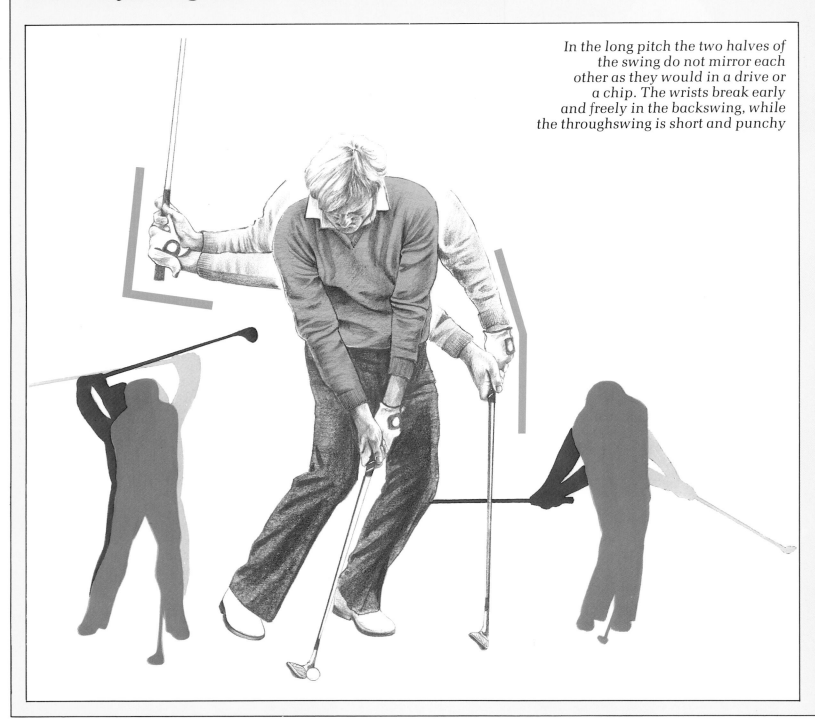

In the long pitch the two halves of the swing do not mirror each other as they would in a drive or a chip. The wrists break early and freely in the backswing, while the throughswing is short and punchy

*When the ball is played back in the
stance, you will meet the ball
earlier than usual in the swing
and probably hit it out to the right
of target. To counteract this,
open your stance by turning your
left foot out slightly*

just as likely to miss to the right as to
the left. It is essential for this kind of
player to build up as definite a routine
when addressing the ball for a pitch
as for a long shot. Because the technique of the shot is fairly simple, low-
handicap golfers – and professionals
– may become slightly careless with
the ball position and produce too
much variation. It is essential to
adopt the same ball position over and
over again. Method in the set-up is as
important in this part of the game as
in any other.

Clubface angle
Another point that is very important is the angle of the clubface at
address. When you move the ball
back in the stance, you often tend to
let the clubface sit in an open position. If you allow the clubface to open
in this way the flight of the ball is
likely to be high and weak, usually
tailing away to the right and finishing
up short of the flag. Check that the
clubface is perfectly square and, for a
more penetrating shot, slightly close
the clubface, attacking the ball well
from the inside in order to keep it
moving through the air.

Most amateur golfers are under the
impression that professional golfers
always pitch the ball with a slightly
cutting action in order to obtain
height and stop – this is just not so.
Many of the best professional golfers
use a sand iron to obtain maximum
height and attack the ball from the
inside with, if anything, the clubface
slightly closed to keep the ball flying
right into the heart of the green. The
ball sits down well once it lands
because of the loft of the club and the

correct downward contact. So, if you
are always ending up short of the flag,
check the line of your swing and the
angle of the clubface.

Varying the distance with these
shots is largely a question of feel and
practice, shortening the backswing
for a shorter shot and combining this
with a fractionally slower attack
through the ball. But remember that
the clubhead must still be acceler-
ating into the back of the ball. If you
try to adapt this long pitch method to
a relatively short shot, do not allow

yourself to swing back too far and
then slow down as you approach the
ball. Always try to limit the length of
the backswing so that you can still
attack the ball forcibly without hitting it too far.

Perhaps this last piece of advice is
what will make most improvement to
your scoring round the golf course.
This is to try to make every pitch shot
you play pass the flag. Make this your
golden rule with pitching and you
will find yourself within one putt distance more and more frequently.

Stroke saving bunker shots

One of the essentials of playing good bunker shots is to possess a good sand wedge. The sort of club most professionals would choose is a club with a rounded leading edge slightly ahead of the hosel and not too large a flange. Avoid a club with a very wry-neck or with a straight leading edge. It can be particularly awkward once you start to try to open the clubface.

The main point to appreciate about the basic splash shot is that the idea is simply to splash out a handful of sand and the ball will pop out with it. You are not actually trying to strike the ball itself. In adopting the address position you should, therefore, place the clubhead as close to the sand as possible and about one-and-a-half or two inches behind the ball. The clubface should be very slightly open in order to increase the possible height. The ball should then be played opposite a spot just inside the left heel with the eyes focused carefully on a little spot in the sand about one-and-a-half inches behind the ball. Whether you like to grip the club right at the end for bunker shots or go down the shaft a couple of inches will most probably depend upon your own height. The address position should then be nice and relaxed with the shaft of the club coming straight up towards you, not with the hands pushed ahead of the ball. The stance should be opened up a little and the swing slightly out-to-in.

The shape of the swing with a bunker shot should be a fairly steep, U-shape. Do not drag the club low along the sand in the backswing, but instead try to have the feeling of almost lifting the club away from the ball to produce the correct steepness. You may find it helps to let the left arm relax slightly in the backswing to produce this U-shape.

Throughout the backswing and the whole of the downswing it is essential to keep the eyes firmly focused on the spot in the sand behind the ball. If you move your eyes from the sand to the ball itself you will almost certainly strike it too cleanly and either thin it into the bunker lip or across the green. So, eyes firmly focused on the spot in the sand, transfer the weight well onto the left foot and concentrate on splashing the clubhead into the correct spot in the sand and then out beyond it.

It is also essential in the down-

Gary Player, probably the world's finest bunker player

An explosion of sand and ball marks this bunker shot by Fuzzy Zoeller

swing to ensure that the weight is transferred onto the left foot without any tendency to fall back onto the right foot in a subconscious attempt to get under the ball and lift it out. The weight must be on the left foot through impact, with the foot and leg movements just as active as in any full shot. It is absolutely vital in the bunker shot to ensure that the clubhead really does go through the sand and out the other side so that you produce a long and relaxed follow-through. The tendency of almost all club golfers is to chop at the sand or to chop at the ball without swinging the club on through. Most players realize the idea of a bunker shot is to enter the sand a couple of inches behind the ball but what they tend to forget is that you must also come out of the sand beyond the ball. If you chop at the ball you are going to produce erratic distance.

What you will find is that it is very much easier to swing the clubhead right through the sand and out the other side into a full follow-through if you keep the speed of the swing very steady, even although this feels ridiculously slow. If you swing the clubhead slowly there is a far greater chance of it penetrating the sand quite smoothly. If you chop at the sand with force and too much speed you will, in fact, compress the sand in such a way that it builds up a great deal of resistance.

The best way of thinking of the importance of slowness is this. If you fire a bullet into sand you will find that the sand compresses and the bullet pulls up in a very short distance. On the other hand, if you

Stroke saving bunker shots

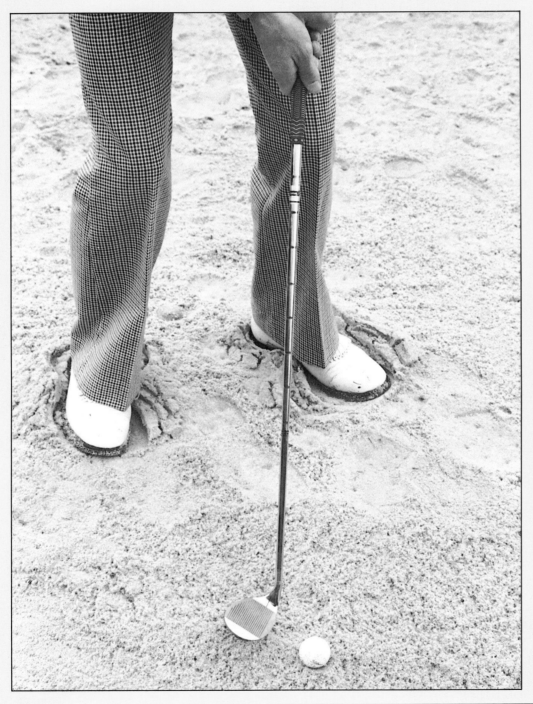

imagine pushing a pencil very smoothly through the sand there would be no resistance at all and the pencil would glide through simply. Just the same applies in a bunker shot: if you chop at the ball the club will stick in the sand, but if you swing slowly the clubhead will pass through easily. Try to play all short bunker shots with a swing that feels almost so slow as to be ridiculous and you will not go far wrong.

Apart from the fault of rushing bunker shots, there are three other pitfalls for the club golfer. The first is the tendency to look away from the spot in the sand and to move the eyes onto the ball itself. If you do this you will almost certainly catch the ball thinly and probably hit it much too far. Once you do this a few times you will tend to lose confidence and probably stop swinging at the ball and sand altogether. So do pick out the little spot in the sand an inch-and-a-half behind the ball and religiously watch this until the shot is over.

The second major cause of problems with bunker shots is the feeling that you want to fall back on the right foot and somehow scoop the ball out of the bunker. It is essential, therefore, to check the end of the swing and to ensure that the body weight has really moved onto the left foot. Subconsciously many golfers try to lift the ball out of the bunker and by dropping back onto the right foot this

Keep the address position relaxed with the shaft coming straight up towards you. The hands should not be ahead of the ball which should be opposite a spot just inside the left heel

somehow gives them the idea that they are going to be able to get under the ball in the throughswing. What will happen here is that the clubhead tends to strike the sand far too far behind the ball producing an unsuitably short shot.

The third fault is one that causes difficulties for all standards of players and is something that low-handicap golfers frequently do without realizing it. Obviously you cannot touch the sand as you address the ball and it is also a breach of the rules to brush any sand on the takeaway. What you should do, however, is to set the clubhead as close to the sand as possible and then ensure that the takeaway and backswing are sufficiently steep to avoid touching the sand. Many players are so conscious of not touching the sand at all that they tend to address the ball with the clubhead

unsuitably high above the sand. Half an inch should be plenty of clearance. Many players will hold the clubhead up to two or three inches above the sand, often without realizing it. If you

To execute the splash shot, place the clubhead as close to the sand as possible, about one and a half or two inches behind the ball

do this it then makes the judgment of the depth, in the down and through-swing, very difficult. You will find that you probably dig much too deep as you go into impact, with very little control of the distance of the shot.

Please remember that the essence of this kind of bunker shot is that you are attempting to splash out the handful of sand and the ball will pop out with it. Keep the swing as slow and full as possible and, above all, do not panic. Because you are simply trying to splash out this handful of sand, the accuracy of contact required with bunker shots is almost less than with many pitches. If you can learn to play good, sound bunker shots this can be an enormous stroke saver.

Judging the length to get the ball close

The professional golfer often astounds the amateur by being able to get the ball very close to the hole with his or her bunker shots. The tournament professional will, in fact, have just as much control from a bunker as with any other shot from around the green. Club golfers should learn to play a shot of approximately ten yards reasonably consistently before being too ambitious at trying to judge the distance. If you cannot hit the ball consistently to one target you are unlikely to be able to vary the distance at will. You will find in addition that a splash shot of ten yards will be very effective from the majority of bunkers around the green. It is a good, sound distance to learn and

From this position, top professionals such as Jack Nicklaus would expect to get the ball very close to the hole

will serve the purpose adequately.

Once you can produce a fairly consistent distance in this way, it is then worthwhile trying to produce different lengths of shot to enable you to get close to the hole within reasonable one putt distance.

There are three different ways in which you can tackle the problem of varying the distance. The first way is to alter the amount you open the clubface. In the standard splash shot, the

Arnold Palmer demonstrates the importance of swinging right through the sand to get the ball out

clubface should be slightly open. If you open the clubface progressively more, you are in effect increasing the loft of the club. This means that for the same length and speed of swing the ball will travel a little higher and a little shorter. If, on the other hand, you play an ordinary splash shot with a square or almost square clubface, you will produce a shot with a slightly lower trajectory and of rather greater length. So this is the first approach – opening or closing the clubface.

The second approach you can use is to vary the amount of sand that you take with the ball. In the ordinary splash shot of about ten yards, the idea would be for the club to enter the sand approximately two inches behind the ball. This would cushion the force of your swing and produce a fairly delicate shot. If you wish to produce an even shorter shot than normal, one way of doing it is to look at the sand further behind the ball – perhaps three or four inches – so that you will cushion the blow even more and produce a shorter shot.

The longer shot

When you wish to produce a longer shot, you can then look at a spot closer to the ball, taking less sand through impact. For a really full shot from a fairway bunker, the ideal is to take the ball completely cleanly. In this case you should look directly at the back of the ball or even slightly towards the top of the ball, which will encourage a clean contact. So, there is the second approach – varying the amount of sand taken and, therefore, the spot you look at in the sand.

Judging the length to get the ball close

With a very open club-face (left) the ball will travel only a short way. If the clubface is less open (centre and right) the ball will go further, with no change necessary in the swing

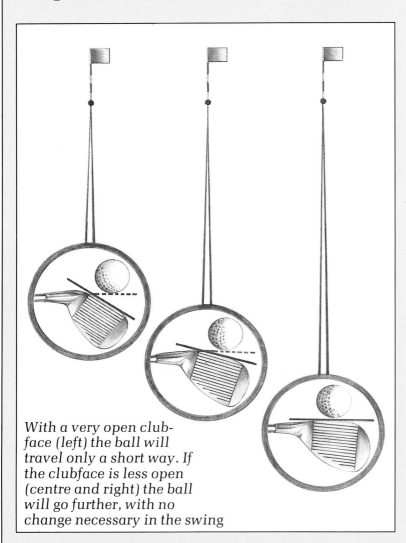

Vary the amount of sand you take with the ball to vary the distance it will go. For a splash shot of ten yards or so, aim to hit the sand about two inches behind the ball(1). For a very short or delicate shot, take more sand, hitting about three or four inches behind the ball(2). For a long shot – out of a fairway bunker, for example – hit the ball cleanly, taking as little sand as possible(3)

The third approach, and by far the most difficult, is to vary the overall length and tempo of the swing to produce the desired shot. This is usually the approach that the tournament professional will use but is definitely not recommended for the amateur golfer. If you try to play a very short shot by cutting down the swing, there is a grave danger of slowing up altogether – quitting on the ball – and failing to get the ball out at all. This shot should be attempted only once you have absolute confidence in your bunker play and know what you are doing. To produce a slightly longer shot, you can swing a little faster and fuller, but the tendency for the club golfer is to rush the shot and lose control. For the majority of tournament professionals the usual approach to playing a very short bunker shot is to cut down the swing and play the shot as slowly and smoothly as possible. This requires perfect timing to execute it correctly. In order to play a longer splash shot of perhaps twenty to thirty yards, the majority of professionals probably square up the clubface and also concentrate on taking slightly less sand.

Summing up

For the club golfer, far the easiest approach to playing a shorter splash shot than normal would be to look at a spot in the sand further behind the ball than usual and simply to hope that you then take more sand, thus cushioning the blow. In order to play a slightly longer shot, adopt an almost square clubface, still looking at a spot in the sand behind the ball but focusing your eyes closer and closer to the ball the longer the shot required. However, the very short bunker shot is the most difficult and it is not something to attempt until you can play a shot of one distance, about ten yards, with reasonable consistency and confidence.

The hardest way to adjust the length of your bunker shots is to adjust the length and speed of your swing. It should be short and slow for the shorter bunker shots, becoming slightly longer and faster as the distance needed increases

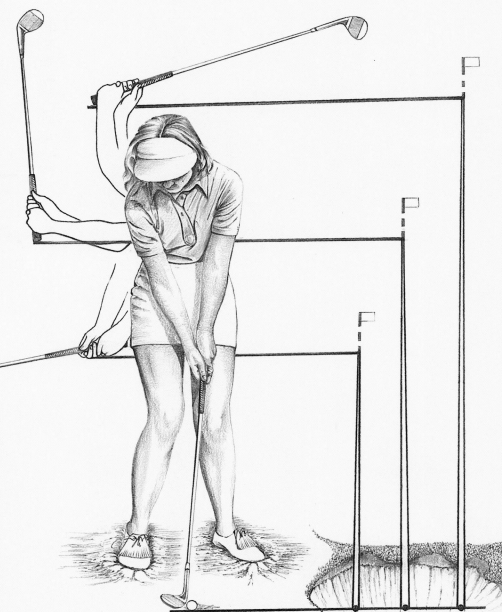

How to hit those tricky downhill shots

Play the ball well back in the stance. The weight should be on the left foot so that the body is at right angles to the slope and with the shoulders following the lie of the slope. The vertical body position on the right is incorrect. This will often cause the player to hit too far behind the ball

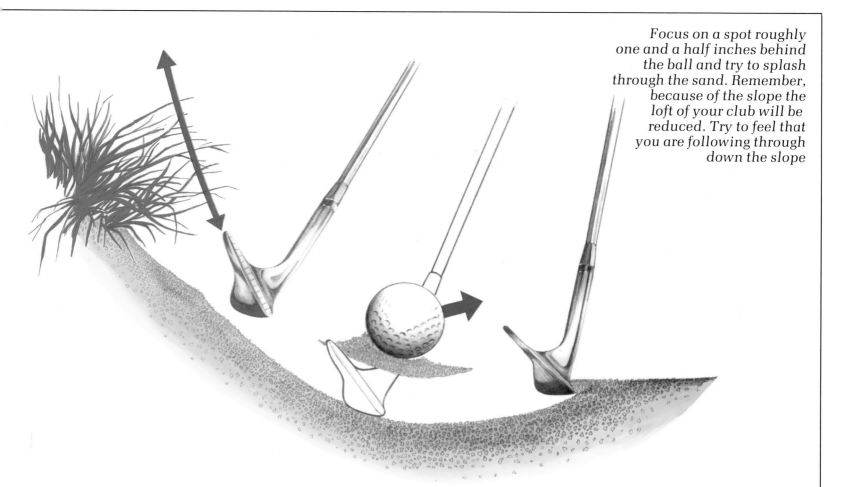

Focus on a spot roughly one and a half inches behind the ball and try to splash through the sand. Remember, because of the slope the loft of your club will be reduced. Try to feel that you are following through down the slope

Probably the most difficult of all the bunker shots is the one that is played from the back of the bunker when the ball has only just trickled into the sand. Whenever you are faced with this kind of problem the ball is usually sitting on some kind of downhill lie which makes the shot extremely difficult to execute.

There are two important points that you should remember about *any* downhill shot. The first thing to appreciate is that the tendency with this type of shot is to catch the ground behind the ball instead of making a fair contact with the ball itself. This is also the case with a bunker shot when the tendency is usually to enter the sand much further back behind the ball than you really intend.

The second point to realize about any downhill shot is that the effective loft of the club is reduced quite considerably so that it is difficult to get much height on the ball.

In order to make it as easy as possible to make a fair contact with the sand and the ball, it is essential to bear two things in mind when setting up. The first one is that the ball should be played well back in the feet, i.e. towards the right foot, which encourages you to make contact with the ball without digging into the sand excessively. The second point is that you should adopt a position where the shoulders *follow the slope of the ground*. In other words, you want to have the weight very much on the left foot with the right shoulder riding very high at address so that the body stands out as far as possible perpendicular to the ground. Once you have got yourself into this position, with the shoulders following the slope of the ground, it is much easier to swing up and down the slope without the tendency to catch the sand unnecessarily deeply behind the ball. This address position may seem awkward

and you will probably feel uncomfortably balanced.

As far as executing the shot is concerned, once you are standing out perpendicular to the slope, your whole idea should be one of swinging the club up and down the slope in much the same way as you would in relation to ordinary flat ground. In the backswing you want an early wrist break, keeping the weight set very much over the left foot so that the backswing is high and steep.

As the downswing takes place, try to keep in mind the idea of swinging *down* the slope rather than trying to scoop the ball upwards into the air. As in all other splash shots, the eyes should be focused throughout the whole swing on a point perhaps one-and-a-half inches behind the ball. This should encourage you to enter the sand in the correct place rather than tending to catch the ball cleanly.

In the downhill bunker shot, try to

How to hit those tricky downhill shots

make the clubhead follow on through the sand beyond the ball rather than lifting on up. You may well find that the balance tends to be lost from a very steep slope so that there is a slight tendency to fall onto the left foot in the throughswing. Provided that you have got the club through the sand, do not worry too much.

Once you can get the feeling of playing the downhill bunker shot in the correct way, and concentrating mainly on keeping the shoulders following the slope of the ground, the execution of the shot should not seem particularly difficult. What you must realize, however, is that the loft of the club is so reduced that the ball will always start off fairly low. Do not imagine that you can get much height from a downhill lie. For this reason it is essential not to be too ambitious in playing a shot from a downhill lie. Do not expect to get the normal height that you would receive usually from an ordinary splash shot.

Whenever you are faced with a downhill lie, try to ascertain the loft that is going to be required to get over the bank which may be between you and the hole. In this kind of situation you must always be prepared to aim away to the side of the flag so that you give yourself less height of bank to overcome, even if it means sacrificing the chance of getting really close to the hole itself by playing out to the side.

Whenever you are playing a downhill bunker shot of this kind, the ball is almost certain to land on the green and run a good ten or fifteen yards after it lands. It makes sense, therefore, for you to aim out to the side of the flag if necessary if it is going to leave you more length of green with which to play.

These, then, are the main essentials for the downhill bunker shot: set the weight very much on the left foot, make the shoulders follow the slope of the ground – keeping the right shoulder very high – look at a spot one-and-a-half to two inches behind the ball and then really concentrate on swinging the club-head *down* the slope in the impact zone.

Even professionals have nightmares about this sort of lie and, as Bernhard Langer shows, concentrate on maintaining their balance

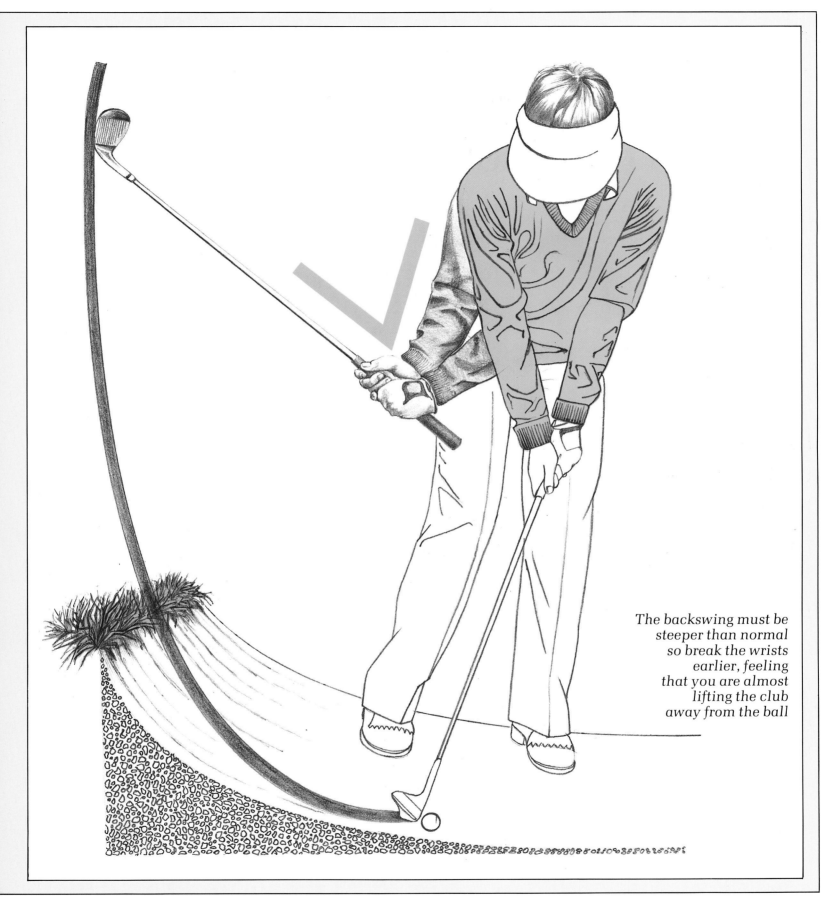

The backswing must be steeper than normal so break the wrists earlier, feeling that you are almost lifting the club away from the ball

How to hole more putts

The first thing to get right is the grip. The putting grip is slightly different to that used in full golf shots. The normal grip for full shots has to control the clubface but it also has to create an abundance of clubhead speed. The thumbs, therefore, are somewhat over the shaft of the putter so as to create the necessary freedom of wrist action.

But in putting you do not need distance as such. You do require the control of distance, and so the grip you use has to be slightly different. The putting grip illustrated here is the one most commonly used by good players and is commonly referred to as the reverse overlap.

As is clearly shown, the last three fingers on the left hand and the first three fingers on the right hand hold the shaft, while the first finger of the left hand overlaps the first three fingers of the right hand.

This grip is not absolutely necessary for good putting but it is important that the palms of the hands are opposite, with the thumbs more or less down the shaft. With the full golf shots the clubface tends to open in the backswing and close in the through-swing; with the palms opposite each other, the clubface can more easily be kept square to the swingpath throughout the stroke.

The stroke

Turning to the stroke itself, it is important to make contact with the

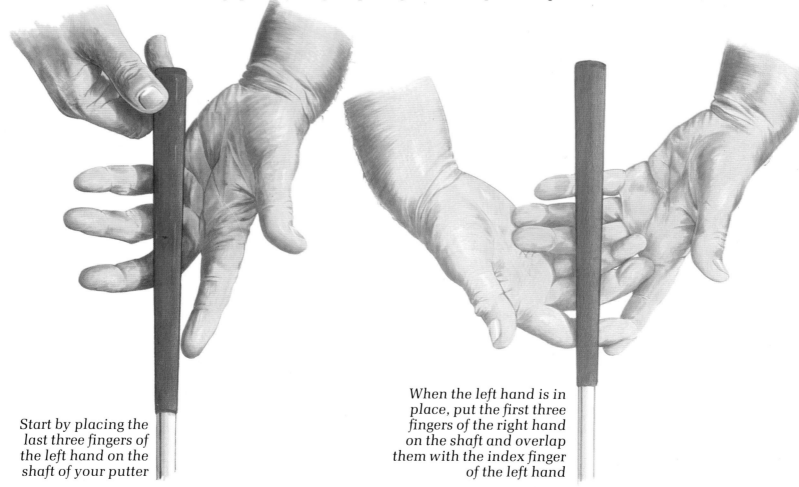

Start by placing the last three fingers of the left hand on the shaft of your putter

When the left hand is in place, put the first three fingers of the right hand on the shaft and overlap them with the index finger of the left hand

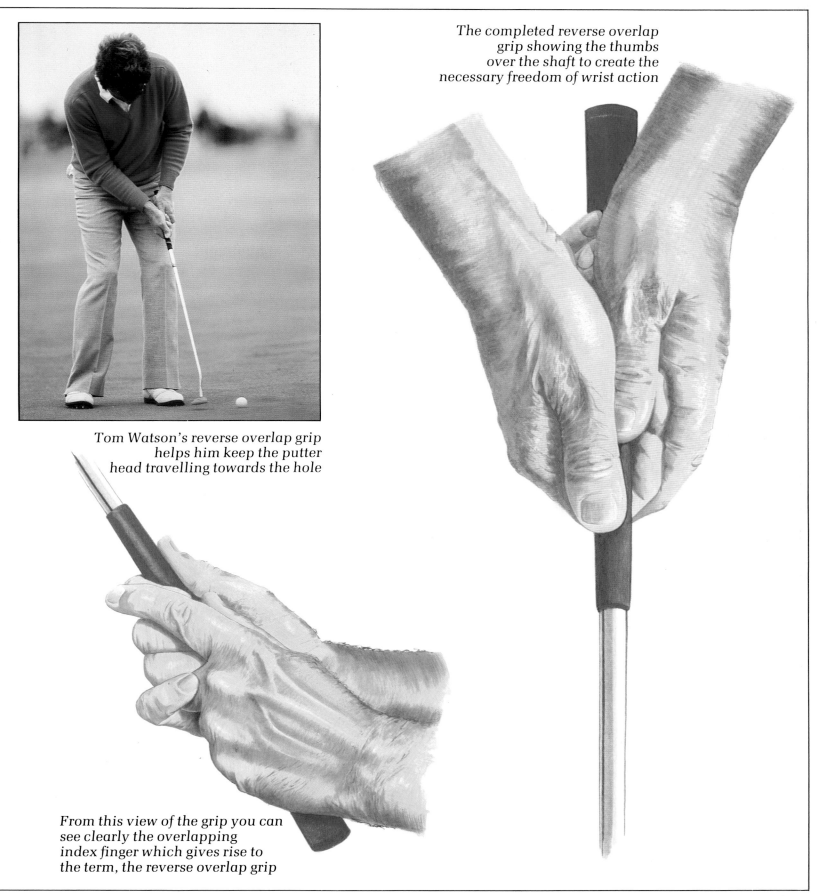

The completed reverse overlap grip showing the thumbs over the shaft to create the necessary freedom of wrist action

Tom Watson's reverse overlap grip helps him keep the putter head travelling towards the hole

From this view of the grip you can see clearly the overlapping index finger which gives rise to the term, the reverse overlap grip

How to hole more putts

clubhead travelling on line and with the clubface square to that line. The fact that the ball is to the side of you necessitates that the clubhead approach the ball from the inside in order for it to be travelling on line, with the face square, at impact.

From inside to straight-through maximizes distance with the long shots – it is the feel of distance for putting. Distance is even more important than direction since a putt other than one that is absolutely straight requires the ball to be rolled at a specific speed in order for it to take the contours in the right proportion.

If you do not consider yourself a good putter you should address the ball in the orthodox manner with the clubface pointing down the line, and the feet, knees, hips and shoulders all parallel to that same line. Whether you swing the putter predominantly with the wrists or arms or shoulders is very much a matter of preference but whichever method you choose must be made easily repetitive. For most of us this usually means a combination of wrist and arm action.

The ball is obviously not very far away from the feet at address and therefore the putter head does not swing in very much but it should be of paramount importance on anything other than the shortest of putts. It would only be true that the putter went straight back from the ball if the lie of the club was such that the shaft would be absolutely perpendicular to the ground.

Many players try to take the putter head straight back from the ball which inevitably forces a hit to the left. Before long these players auto-

matically react with a quick opening of the clubface at impact. This action is often referred to as the 'yips'. It comes about through a misconception of the desired arc which will then *release* the putter head along the desired line.

The correct length of swing should be one that creates the necessary putter head acceleration through the ball; too long a swing will obviously decelerate at impact whereas a too short backswing has the effect of a sudden acceleration devoid of feel and often resulting in excess body movement which in itself throws the putter head off line. If you are suffering on the greens, practise using a swing distinctly longer or shorter than you have been doing. This often leads to a realization that the swing has not been of the desired length.

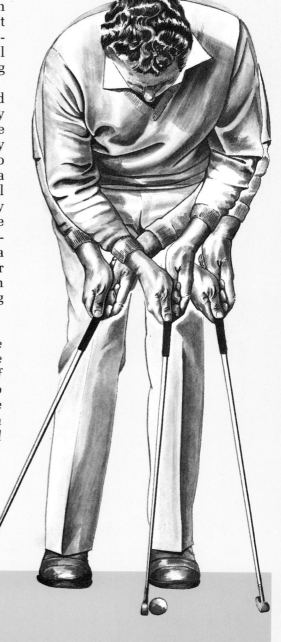

This illustration shows the ball not far away from the feet. The correct length of swing varies from player to player but it must create putter head acceleration through the ball

1

2

3

4

5

6

The legendary putting stroke of Severiano Ballesteros combines sound fundamentals with tremendous touch. At address(1) he is relaxed and concentrating on the line he wishes the ball to take. Starting the backswing(2) with a smooth takeaway there is no sign of wrist break as he completes the backswing(3). Approaching the ball(4) with the left wrist leading and the blade square to the line. Just after impact(5) and the head has remained still and only starts to come up(6) well after the ball is on its way

Two keys to better putting

When talking about putting there are two distinct elements involved. One is reading the green in order to be able to set the ball off at the right pace and in the right direction, and the other is the development of a sound stroke to facilitate correct striking of the ball.

The great putters have the gift of being able to read the line and see the way into the hole. This ability to read greens can be a tremendous asset, of course. We have all had days when we are able to see the line and it is on these occasions that all of us putt well. We become very positive with our stroke. Conversely, when we are not sure what the ball is going to do this doubt has its effect on our striking of the ball. Jack Nicklaus is a great reader of greens and his penchant for fast greens reflects his confidence in being able to read the line, which, of course, is so much more important when greens are particularly fast. Nicklaus is also known not to be fond of slow greens; his very address position, with the ball particularly forward in the stance, gives the impression that he finds it easy to set putts off in the right direction coupled with his wonderful feel for pace.

In terms of how we lesser mortals should approach this problem of the line, we can only look from behind the ball to the hole and from the hole back to the ball and form a judgment as to how the green is going to affect the roll of the putt. Some days you can do this and be quite confident that you are correct in your judgment. It is on these occasions when you are not sure, that it is *vital to commit yourself to a line* and make sure you set the ball off along it with complete authority. This is of vital importance on the short putts, i.e. those from two to eight feet. To be still hesitant about

the line when you are striking the ball is fatal. Most of us when we are practising short putts are quite good, since after the first two putts we know the

Gary Player demonstrates his great putting skill

line and therefore everything is much easier. *Commit yourself to a line before you strike the ball.*

In terms of the stroke, it should be one that makes contact with the club travelling along the desired line with the clubface square to it. Dealing with the clubface first, it is important that your palms are opposite each other with the back of the left hand square to the line. This helps to keep the clubface square to the swingpath throughout the stroke. With the longer shots, the left hand is turned over the shaft to some extent, which allows the clubface to open in the backswing and close in the through-swing. This is necessary since, with the longer shots, we are not only looking for direction but also much more power. To achieve an impact with the clubhead travelling along the line it is necessary on all but the shortest of putts for the clubhead to approach the ball on an arc slightly from the inside.

The forward press

Those of you who are familiar with the putting methods of many of the American circuit players, who as a group must surely be the best in the world, will have recognized that many of them have a forward press immediately before taking the putter back from the ball. Many would stress that this is to give them a firm left wrist at impact which helps to keep the clubface square through the ball. However, this forward press has the added advantage of directing the putter head back on the desired slightly inside arc.

In practice terms, a club shaft

When putting you may choose to adopt the reverse overlap grip. The index finger of the left hand overlaps the fingers of the right

should be laid along the ground and the ball should be positioned close enough to it so that a measurable distance of, say, one inch is left between the toe of the putter and the shaft of the club on the ground. It will be found that if the putter head is taken back the correct amount on the inside (and it is relatively little) when the ball has been struck, the putter head will finish with the toe of the club the same one inch from the shaft. When this is achieved you know the club-head is swinging through the ball in the correct direction. On long putts the putter head will, of course, return slightly to the inside and will finish its arc further from the shaft on the ground than the original position.

Winter evenings spent practising indoors, with the hands warm are far better than when the hands are cold during outdoor practice at that time of the year.

Practise medium and long-distance putts since if this element is good there will not be such a strain on short putts. All the good putters are marvellous at rolling the long ones absolute-

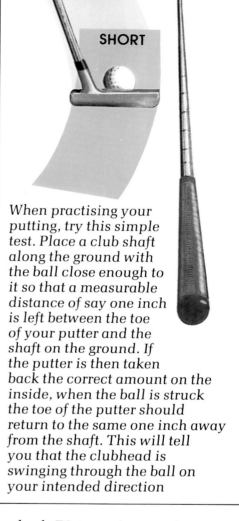

When practising your putting, try this simple test. Place a club shaft along the ground with the ball close enough to it so that a measurable distance of say one inch is left between the toe of your putter and the shaft on the ground. If the putter is then taken back the correct amount on the inside, when the ball is struck the toe of the putter should return to the same one inch away from the shaft. This will tell you that the clubhead is swinging through the ball on your intended direction

ly dead. Distance is more important than direction since other than on a perfectly flat green there is no line to the hole unless you can hit the ball at a particular pace.

Summing up then, practise lots of long putts and if the strike is from inside to straight through, this releasing of the putter head along the line is a great help in feeling the distance. Develop this inside to straight through stroke by practising with a shaft on the ground or, if indoors, by hitting putts parallel to the skirting board in a warm room. And on short putts never strike the ball without first committing yourself to the line.

Lining up on the greens

Because you stand to the side of the ball and its intended direction, it is always difficult to aim the club correctly at the target. Theoretically, this difficulty should be reduced greatly when you are using a putter because the eyes should be positioned directly over the ball, and judging a straight line should therefore be easier. However, many golfers still have problems in looking sideways at the hole and aiming correctly.

Here is a simple way to test whether you are aiming correctly. Set yourself up on your living-room carpet with an inverted tee-peg forming your target and a golf ball placed about six feet away from this. Now place a very small coin directly on line between the ball and the target, about two feet from the ball. If you now resume your address position you may well find that the three objects do not appear to be in a straight line. If the coin seems to be to the left then you are probably aiming off to the right. Conversely, if the coin appears to be to the right then you are aiming off to the left. If all three objects appear in a straight line then your aim is correct. If your aim is either left or right, then simply adjust your stance and head position until the three objects appear in line. Repeating this test constantly will eventually give you the right feel for lining up when you are next on the course, and may be the answer to your putting problems.

Lining up the putter shaft with the ball and the hole is referred to as plumb-bobbing and is used to determine which way a putt will break

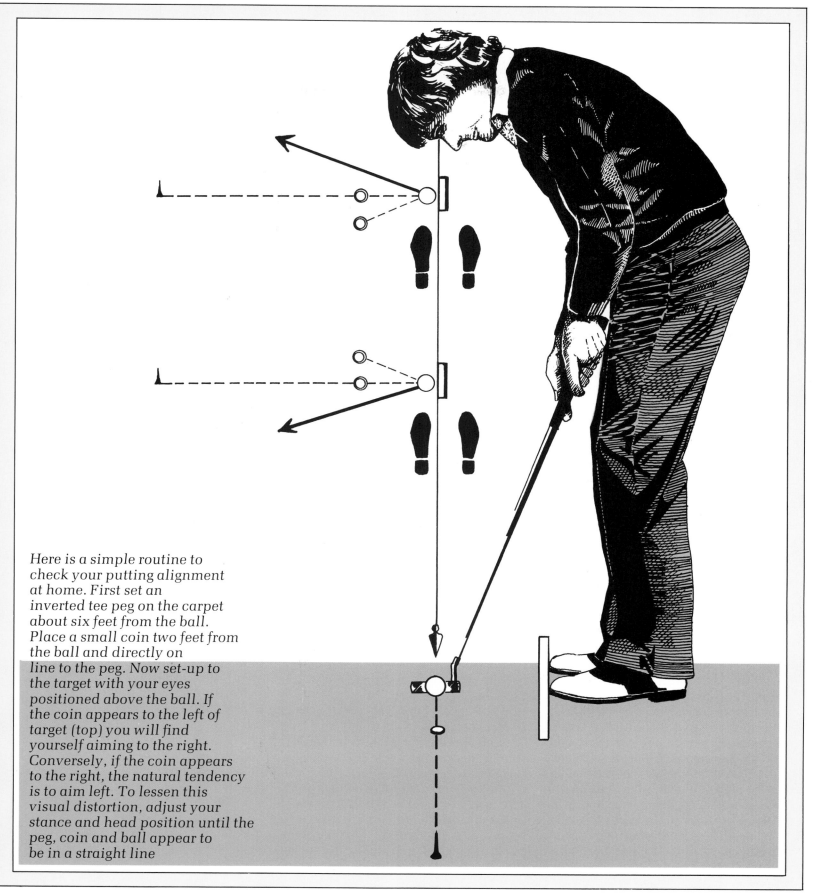

Here is a simple routine to check your putting alignment at home. First set an inverted tee peg on the carpet about six feet from the ball. Place a small coin two feet from the ball and directly on line to the peg. Now set-up to the target with your eyes positioned above the ball. If the coin appears to the left of target (top) you will find yourself aiming to the right. Conversely, if the coin appears to the right, the natural tendency is to aim left. To lessen this visual distortion, adjust your stance and head position until the peg, coin and ball appear to be in a straight line

Every golfer, at sometime or other, is afflicted by a particular kind of bad shot. Knowing what causes these bad shots can help you to eradicate them. This chapter analyses the cause and effect of bad shots and provides you with the steps to cure them. Here, you can discover why the slice and the pull are closely related, why golfers who push the ball are also liable to hook it, how to stop topping plus a cure for that most dreaded of golfing ailments – the shank. Learn how to avoid an overswing and dismiss the myth of the late hit. Whatever bad shot ails you, this chapter provides an easy-to-assimilate cure which will soon have you hitting the ball correctly and with renewed confidence.

The slice

The most common swing fault among golfers is undoubtedly the one that produces a left-to-right flight on the golf ball – in other words, a slice. You must understand at the outset that any shots that curve to the right are struck with the clubface open. This invariably leads to an aim off to the left, conscious or otherwise, allowing for the shot. This aiming off to the left leads also to an out-to-in steep, open-faced impact resulting in shots lacking in power which start left and curve to the right. The direct control of the clubface is dependent on the way in which you hold the club. In the simplest of terms, you are endeavouring to hold it at address in a position you will be in at impact.

Golfers with a tendency to slice need to have the 'V's between the thumb and first finger of both hands pointing towards the right shoulder. Although the grip is the direct control of the clubface, it is not the only control. There are many golfers with very strong hookers' grips who still manage to slice consistently. The swing path itself also has a tremendous bearing on the clubface. Once again, you should remember that you are playing a game with the ball positioned to the side of you. It follows then that the arc of swing will be from the inside to straight through at impact and inside again on the follow-through. This type of arc through the ball will allow the clubface to close in sympathy with the arc. A left-to-right flight of the ball indicates that the clubface is open and the swing path itself is out-to-in.

At address, slicers invariably position the ball too far forwards in the stance, which means that the ball will be struck on the follow-through side of the arc when the clubhead is travelling well left of the target. This arc will automatically block any closing of the clubface, since over-riding all attempts to swing the club correctly will be an involuntary blocking of the hands in a vain attempt to propel the ball in the desired direction. This blocking action will, in effect, leave the clubface open even if the grip itself is correct.

At address the ball needs to be positioned far enough back in the stance, towards the right foot, to allow the shoulders to be square or even closed. The hands should be slightly forward of the clubhead, *which will appear to be fractionally open.* This address position makes it possible to swing the club into the ball from the inside,

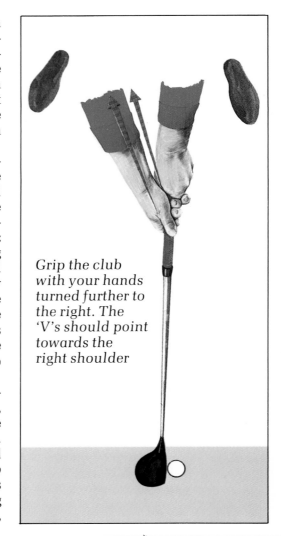

Grip the club with your hands turned further to the right. The 'V's should point towards the right shoulder

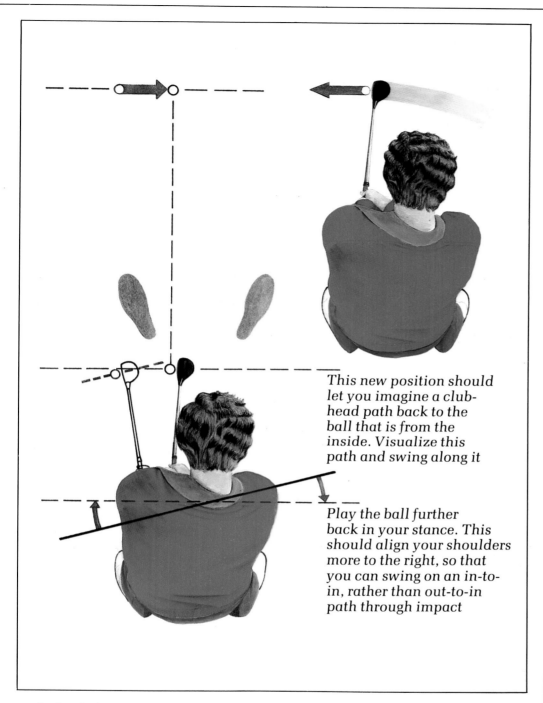

Although the clubface is square at address, the slicer will return it to the ball in an open position with the arc of the swing blocking any closing of the clubface

This new position should let you imagine a club-head path back to the ball that is from the inside. Visualize this path and swing along it

Play the ball further back in your stance. This should align your shoulders more to the right, so that you can swing on an in-to-in, rather than out-to-in path through impact

If rolling the clubface open is your problem (white arrow), then keep the clubface looking at the ball for a while during the first part of the backswing on an inside path

with the hands and arms, since the swing path can be visualized before the club is moved.

The reaction of this approach of the club to the ball will be one of clearing the hips out of the way, thus allowing the clubhead to move from the inside to straight through to the target. The clubface, open in the downswing, will square up at impact.

To sum up, if your long shots tend to start to the left and slice away to the right, then position the ball further back in your stance and close your shoulder position. Make sure that your grip is one with both 'V's pointing to the right shoulder. Swing the club down from the top with the hands and arms from the inside, clearing the hips in unison with the downward swing of the club. Swing from the inside and clear the left side.

The hook

The hook is often referred to as the good golfer's bad shot and while there may be some truth in that, it is also possibly the most destructive of bad shots in terms of landing the ball in deep trouble. In curing a hook it is important to be reminded of the inter-relationship between the clubface, swing path and angle of approach of the club to the ball. Of these three impact factors, the clubface is by far the most important since if this is in-correct it will affect the other two adversely, too.

All shots that hook bend in the air to the left and are struck with the clubface closed at impact. This type of flight, creating fear of going to the left in the player's mind, invariably leads to an in-to-out swing path. This swing path leads to an upward hit through the ball. In other words, the bottom of the arc arrives too early, that is, behind the ball. This type of action is usually fairly successful when the ball is teed up, particularly if there is enough loft on the club to obviate the closed clubface. However, with the bottom of the arc behind the ball, any shot from off the ground becomes very difficult, particularly when the ball is lying 'tight'. The flight of the ball, which is a direct reflection of the clubface position at impact, has a real bearing on the swing arc that we all use. Much swing instruction ignores this vital fact. The perfect swing arc does not hit good shots unless the clubface is also cor-rect at the moment of impact. This is why so many players claim good practice swings, since with no ball the clubface element of the swing is totally ignored. There are two ways in which the clubface is affected: direct-ly by the grip; and, secondly, by the

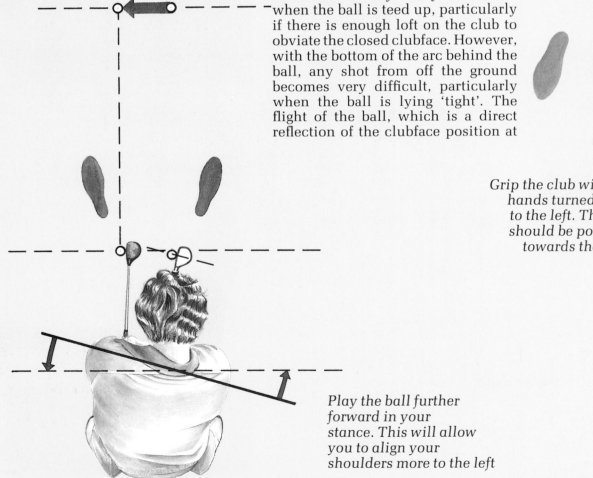

Grip the club with the hands turned more to the left. The 'V's should be pointing towards the chin

Play the ball further forward in your stance. This will allow you to align your shoulders more to the left

Hit some practice shots with your bottom close up to a wall or bush. This will eliminate a flat swing plane, otherwise you will hit the barrier

Clear your left side and your arms can swing freely down and forward on the desired in-to-in arc squaring the clubface on impact

swing path itself. Golf is made more difficult because when things go wrong our natural reaction is apt to make things worse.

When shots begin to bend to the left, often because of a faulty grip, we react by swinging the club into the ball too much from the inside. This, in itself, creates extensive wrist roll which tends to close the clubface even more. A hook, then, is hit with the clubface closed with the swing path approaching too much inside, with the bottom of the arc behind the ball. Therefore, our first endeavour must be to get the clubface square.

Those players with the ability to accelerate the clubhead usually need to grip the club in what is described as a 'weak' position; that is, with both 'V's between the thumb and first finger of each hand pointing to the chin. If you hook the ball, this is the

first step to getting the clubface square. You should also make the pressure on the grip the same in both hands. If the left hand is tighter than the right, the right wrist will become too active in the hitting area relative to the arms, thus closing the clubface.

When shots are bent consistently from right to left, then it is probable that the set-up is closed and the aim is to the right of the target. The ball then should be positioned further forward in the stance, towards the left foot, and the right foot and shoulder advanced to create a feeling of being more open. It must be remembered that the grip is not in isolation of the other set-up factors and that this more open set-up will encourage a weaker grip. From this address position, it is important in the downswing to combine a feeling of swinging the club down at the same time that the left

side is cleared. Initially, to anyone who has been hooking shots, the swing path will feel out-to-in and, therefore, the bottom of the arc much further forwards than hitherto. The basic function of the backswing is to get the club shaft in a correct position relative to the target. It is important to consciously swing the club up on to the target in the backswing as opposed to just pivoting and allowing the club to follow the shoulder turn too closely resulting in a flat arc of swing which also tends to close the clubface at impact.

To sum up, at address weaken the grip, position the ball more forward in the stance and feel the shoulders and feet are more open. From this position, concentrate, in the backswing, on swinging the club up on to the target and, as the club is swung down, clear the left side.

How to avoid skying

Skying is not one of the most common faults but it is something that almost every player experiences at some time or another. It is extremely annoying to watch the ball soar skywards, possibly travelling twice as high as forwards, particularly as the shot is usually straight.

A skied ball is clearly the opposite of a topped shot, and as a topped shot occurs when the clubface is above the ball at impact, so a skied shot occurs when contact has been made with too much clubface below the centre of the ball. There is a simple reason for this and, in essence, it is because the clubhead is picked up sharply at the start of the swing outside the intended line of flight and is then chopped across on the downswing from outside-to-in. Through snatching the clubhead up and away there is little or no pivot. The action gives a steep backswing, and chop down into the ball must follow. Trying to hit the ball further than is humanly possible is one of the causes of a steep pick-up so it is important to remember that the club must be swung smoothly and the clubhead kept low to the ground at the start of the swing.

Skying can occur also if the player keeps too much weight on the left foot during the backswing. This will cause the left shoulder to dip, and a steep, narrow backswing will result. To prevent this, make sure your weight is distributed evenly at address and start the backswing by keeping the clubhead low to the turf for the first twelve inches.

Remember that in order to get the ball travelling forwards, the clubhead must approach the ball parallel to the ground several inches before the ball is struck, and it is the loft of the clubface that will propel the ball upwards. Many players feel that they have to help the ball upwards with a 'scooping' action and throw the clubhead at the ball from the top of the swing. This action makes the clubhead pass the hands before impact and thus it produces contact below the centre of the ball.

When using a driver, it does not always follow that teeing the ball high produces a skied shot. The average player does not sky the ball from a high tee but the chronic skier will sky

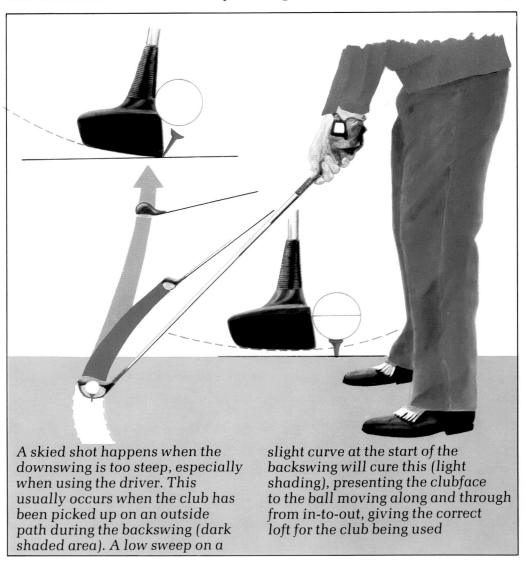

A skied shot happens when the downswing is too steep, especially when using the driver. This usually occurs when the club has been picked up on an outside path during the backswing (dark shaded area). A low sweep on a slight curve at the start of the backswing will cure this (light shading), presenting the clubface to the ball moving along and through from in-to-out, giving the correct loft for the club being used

Throwing the clubhead from the top contributes to skying and is usually brought about by slogging or scooping. At impact the weight is forced back on to the right side, the right shoulder drops and the right hand 'flaps' under with the result that extra loft is added to the clubface and power is reduced

a shot from either a low or a high tee. In fact, players with a steep angle of attack into the ball will invariably tee the ball low as they feel that, with a high tee, the club will pass right underneath the ball. Players who do this should tee the ball higher and try and sweep it away with the clubhead travelling nearer the ground on the backswing and throughswing and on an in-to-out path. Skying is a close companion of the slice and is caused by a narrow, steep swing arc. If you widen and flatten that arc then the problem will be eradicated.

How to cure the push

The push is often regarded as the good golfer's error as it occurs when the club is swung on an exaggerated in-to-out track with the clubface square to that line. In producing the push, the golfer has achieved many of the correct movements required for good striking but has probably moved the body ahead of the ball before it is struck.

There are two main causes of this: firstly, a sway to the left on the downswing which is due to the player not releasing the clubhead through the hitting area; and, secondly, addressing the ball too far back towards the right foot.

When a player sways to the left, generally starting halfway on the downswing, both his body and hands are positioned ahead of the ball at impact. The clubface has no chance of squaring up to the intended line of flight. Should the swing be on an in-to-out track the ball will fly straight to the right. With this type of pushed shot, the clubface will eventually reach the square position a few inches after the ball has been struck.

A sway to the left can be caused also by swaying to the right on the backswing. The sway to the left is by way of compensation and the player usually overdoes it. Once again, this puts the hands and body ahead of the ball at impact.

Curing a sway

To stop a sway on the backswing make sure the clubhead starts round on an inclined plane. This makes the body rotate and thus it will not move out of the space it occupies at the time of address. In addition, make sure

that you start to release the clubhead during the first part of the downswing so that it will be freewheeling past you. At impact it will have reached maximum speed and will have become almost an independent body. Sometimes a player may have a good backswing and still sway into the ball. This generally happens when the hands have tightened up, usually through anxiety. The clubhead cannot be released and the player takes the clubhead through the shot with a body sway to the left. But if the swing is in-to-out, a push to the right results and sometimes the ball is half-topped.

Wrong ball position

A pushed shot can result also without any sway should the ball be positioned too far to the right of centre in the stance. Then the clubface will meet the ball before it has time to square up correctly at the bottom of the swing arc, which, during a proper swing, is always left of centre.

It follows, therefore, that by having the ball positioned to the right of centre at address the body and hands will naturally be ahead of the ball at impact. The effect is exactly the same as playing the ball from the accepted position and swaying to the left on the downswing. In each case the clubface presents itself to the ball – with an in-to-out swing – square to the direction the club is following but open to the intended target line. Another cause of pushing is through a flat inside backswing. The player swinging on a flat plane rolls the clubface open (clockwise), which means it will be wide

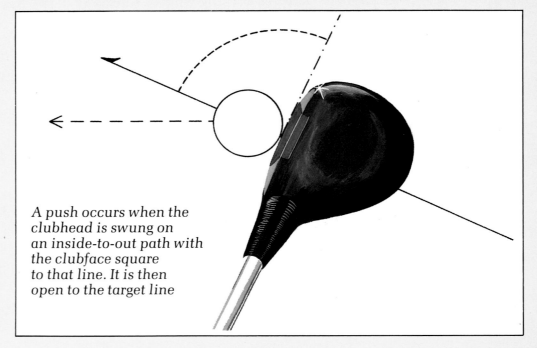

A push occurs when the clubhead is swung on an inside-to-out path with the clubface square to that line. It is then open to the target line

If a player sways to the left on the downswing, his body and hands will be in front of the club at impact with the clubface open. The swing's axis moves to the left, causing a half-topped shot to the right, with the bottom of the swing occurring forward of the ball position

To stop swaying to the left on the way back to the ball, release the clubhead sooner or try to get the clubhead to the ball first. This gives maximum speed at impact together with a square clubface

open at the top of the backswing.

When this takes place, the player may not roll it back square to impact. So the face is still open and usually with a flat backswing, returns to the ball from inside-to-out. In trying to square up the clubface, the player rolls the clubhead to extreme proportions and a hook or a smother results.

The remedy for this is to start the swing by making certain the club starts back on an inside path close to the turf, keeping the clubface looking at the ball for a while. This will automatically make the backswing more upright which helps make the swing a little straighter than the shot. Finally, check your grip to make sure that it is not in a weak position – with one or both hands too far round to the left. Should they be in this position even when swinging correctly, you are likely to produce an open clubface through the shot.

Toeing – the causes and the remedies

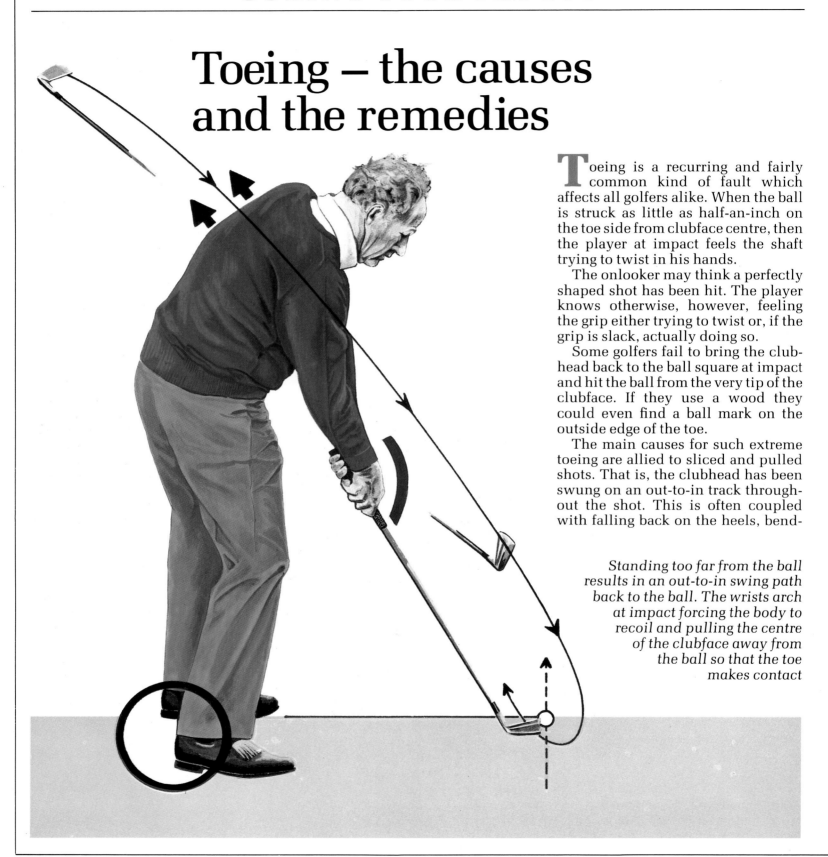

Toeing is a recurring and fairly common kind of fault which affects all golfers alike. When the ball is struck as little as half-an-inch on the toe side from clubface centre, then the player at impact feels the shaft trying to twist in his hands.

The onlooker may think a perfectly shaped shot has been hit. The player knows otherwise, however, feeling the grip either trying to twist or, if the grip is slack, actually doing so.

Some golfers fail to bring the clubhead back to the ball square at impact and hit the ball from the very tip of the clubface. If they use a wood they could even find a ball mark on the outside edge of the toe.

The main causes for such extreme toeing are allied to sliced and pulled shots. That is, the clubhead has been swung on an out-to-in track throughout the shot. This is often coupled with falling back on the heels, bend-

Standing too far from the ball results in an out-to-in swing path back to the ball. The wrists arch at impact forcing the body to recoil and pulling the centre of the clubface away from the ball so that the toe makes contact

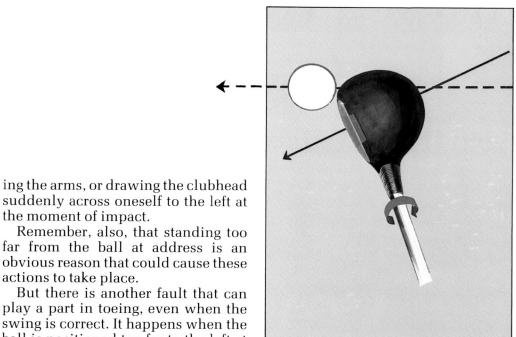

Hitting the ball off the toe is caused by an exaggerated out-to-in swing or by standing too far from the ball, and even a combination of both. When this takes place, the player feels the club trying to twist clockwise in his hands

ing the arms, or drawing the clubhead suddenly across oneself to the left at the moment of impact.

Remember, also, that standing too far from the ball at address is an obvious reason that could cause these actions to take place.

But there is another fault that can play a part in toeing, even when the swing is correct. It happens when the ball is positioned too far to the left at address for the club to be used. The ball will then be struck *after* the bottom of the swing arc has been passed, by which time the club has started its journey around to the finish of the swing.

If you combine the positioning error with any one of the three toeing faults as described, that only serves to magnify the trouble – and you can start looking for those white marks on the toe of your woods.

Most players who toe shots do so as a result of a poor backswing. A similar action causes the pull and slice. The clubhead has been picked up on the outside at the start of the swing, which in turn restricts the left shoulder from turning a full 90 degrees. From this incorrect top of the backswing position, the clubhead will move along a line back to the ball left of the intended line of flight, which is the exact opposite to the circumstances of a shank, when the club is swung too much from in-to-out, combined with a stiff action.

The distance you stand from the ball before playing any shot is of great importance. A large percentage of golfers do tend to stand too far from the ball at address. To them this feels a powerful position. But it will only

make them swing back and through on a flat plane in a scythe-like action. The player has to reach out to make contact with the ball and this brings about loss of power.

Centrifugal force, which is a natural force that recedes from the centre happens with anything that is moving in a circular direction or motion. In golf, at impact, this force is at its maximum and makes the wrist arch and the body stretch.

Centrifugal force can have opposing effects on any shot according to the swing path involved. If the swing is too much in-to-out then the effect of centrifugal force is to make the clubhead move away from the player, and the danger here is that the socket could be sent into the ball. It means, of course, that the clubhead is travelling away from the player.

On the other hand, if the swing should be too much out-to-in, then the reverse can occur. The player recoils backwards and straightens his back a little as the clubhead comes into the ball. It means he will be pulling the centre of the clubface away from the ball and striking the shot off the toe.

So it is easy to recognize by this that it is most important to stand your

correct distance from the ball for the particular club being used, neither too near nor too far. The correct distance will make you swing slightly under yourself and a little on an inclined plane. That is exactly what we are seeking. For how to assess your correct distance, turn to the section on shanking. The over-correction outlined there is designed to help the player to feel the centre of the clubface once again. If this cure is actually overdone it results in the ball being struck off the toe.

So when you think about it, you can see that the cure for toeing is to make the clubhead move on a line inside-to-out. Or, as an over-correction, swing the clubhead out to the right of the intended line of flight. Overdone, of course, the ball could well be struck off the heel. Practice is the answer to achieve that fine adjustment.

In order to reach a correct top of the backswing position, so allowing the player to swing back to the ball from in-to-out, start the backswing round on an inclined plane. This will make the left shoulder turn a full 90 degrees and arrive under the chin by the time the top of the backswing is reached. From such a position, make the clubhead follow exactly the same path by swinging back to the ball and through the whole lot.

But beware. Even if the top of the backswing is correct, it is still possible to hit across the ball by throwing the clubhead out on an outside line in which case, the same cure, just described, will apply.

Assuming that the grip, stance, backswing, and position of the ball at address are correct, then the ball can

Toeing – the causes and the remedies

With the correct swing it is still possible to toe the ball if you position the ball too far to the left. The bottom of the arc has been passed and the clubhead is already moving inside. The dotted line shows the proper ball position still be struck off the toe through the arms bending just before impact or by falling back a little onto the heels. Keeping the weight on the right foot too long can produce a similar result.

What causes such faulty body movements? As always stated, all body actions or reactions are a direct result of how the clubhead has been swung. One of the main villains of the toeing complaint is our old familiar friend – slogging in an attempt to get extra distance. However, what you need in golf is *swinging power* – not powerful effort – when you are making a stroke.

Another major cause of toeing, when it comes to the high handicapper, is an instinctive fear of not being able to get the ball airborne. Subconsciously the player tries to help the loft on the clubface by scooping at the ball. When this happens, his body reacts naturally by straightening and then falling back on to the right foot with both arms bending.

To overcome scooping, always trust the loft built into the clubface when playing a shot, and imagine you are going to drive the ball low under a tree. The loft on the clubface will give the desired elevation for the club being used, and the body actions, in response, will look after themselves, taking on a new correct form without you trying to make them happen.

As that great teacher of the game, the late Ernest Jones, wrote: "The body and all its parts should be treated as disastrous leaders but as wholly admirable followers of any clubhead swung on the correct path."

Corrections for toeing

1 Check your grip and stance.
2 Check the position of the ball at address, making sure that it is in the correct position for the club being used.
3 Check you are not standing too far away from the ball at address.

To stop a scooping action imagine you are playing the ball under an overhanging tree and drive it along and through. This picture of Jerry Pate is an excellent example of this desired action

4 Check the start of the backswing. The golf swing is more or less a circle and must start with this in mind in order to form one.

5 Check the top of the backswing. The left shoulder should be tucked under the chin.

6 Make the downswing start inside the intended line of flight.

7 Do not slog. Swing the clubhead back to the ball. Swinging creates centrifugal force. This will naturally stop your arms from bending through impact. It also checks falling back on the heels and gives correct weight transference and balance.

8 Resist the temptation to help the ball into the air. Drive it down, forward and through.

The solid figure shows a comfortable address position the correct distance from the ball. The dotted image is standing too far from the ball. Start the swing by making the clubhead stay close to the turf on a slight curve for about ten to fifteen inches. The two clubheads at the top show the respective positions at the top of the backswing

How to avoid topping

Topping is particularly common to beginners but many experienced players occasionally hit the ball straight along the ground at the most inappropriate time. Nothing is more annoying. When you address the ball before swinging you establish a certain distance between yourself and the bottom of the ball. You measure this distance with your left arm and the golf club as you set it on the ground behind the ball. The arm and club combined form the radius of the swing. But during the backswing this radius is shortened considerably because of the cocking of the wrists, and unless in the downswing the wrists are fully uncocked, the original radius will not be re-established. The clubhead just cannot get back to the bottom of the ball.

There has been much stress of leg and body action over the past two decades, and this is understandable since much of this type of advice emanates from the great players. They all swing the club freely with the arms and hands in the downswing and are apt to assume that lesser mortals do likewise. Unfortunately this is not always the case; over-emphasis of body action in the downswing and the clubhead fails to catch up. The wrists are still cocked to some extent when the ball is reached. The beginner's first priority should be to re-establish the swing radius similar to that at address by impact. We

The left arm and club combine forming a radius for the swing

During the backswing you lose a large part of this radius due to the wristcock

If the wrists do not fully uncock, the clubhead does not get back to the bottom of the ball ▶

measure ourselves from the ball at address, and the downswing is a re-measuring of this radius. It also happens to be the striking of the ball with the clubhead — the whole essence of the game.

When shots are frequently topped because the wrists are not fully uncocked there will also be a tendency for the ball to slice since the clubface will be left open. Therefore, follow a practice drill with a relatively easy club such as a 6-iron or a 3-wood with

In the downswing the wrists must fully uncock to re-establish the original radius of the address position

the ball teed appropriately, concentrating on reaching the bottom of the arc behind the ball. This sort of thinking retards body action in the downswing and increases the use of the arms and hands so as to arrive at impact with the club shaft and left arm in a relatively straight line at or before impact thus reaching the bottom of the ball with the clubhead.

It should be remembered that the golf swing is a combination of hand and arm action and body action. What is suggested will increase the use of arms and hands and nullify to some extent the application of the body to the ball (usually the shoulders) as opposed to the clubhead. When the ground is being hit consistently behind the ball, obviously you should then begin to focus on the ball itself rather than behind it.

How to stop hitting behind the ball

Hitting the ground behind the ball, or hitting 'fat' as it is popularly known, is a common fault among golfers. To correct this fault, you must remember that the golf swing is a balance of the correct hand and arm action and body action. These elements must be synchronized to obtain the best results. When the ground is being hit behind the ball, the hands and arms will be working from the top independently of the body and, therefore, the radius of the swing (that is the left arm and club shaft) will reach its maximum too early in the downswing. This over-wide downswing will tend to make contact with the ground before you are ready for it.

This action tends to produce hooked shots since the clubhead will have passed the hands and will be closed by the time the ball is reached. To correct this, the player should concentrate on unwinding the lower half of the body at the same time that the arms swing down. Every attempt should be made to keep the legs and hips active so that the hips can be more open to the target before the ball is actually struck.

Many golfers with these particular faults, hitting behind and hooking, have made a conscious effort to grip very lightly with the right hand. The effect of this is for the right wrist to become too active at the top of the backswing leading to a casting action which creates excessive width on the downswing. It is important to grip the club with the same pressure in both hands to avoid separating the hands at the top.

To prevent this separation, practise with a blade of grass placed on top of the left thumb and, with the right palm in place, swing through the ball without dislodging the grass. Even the great professionals like Gary Player have been helped by this suggestion which has improved their game.

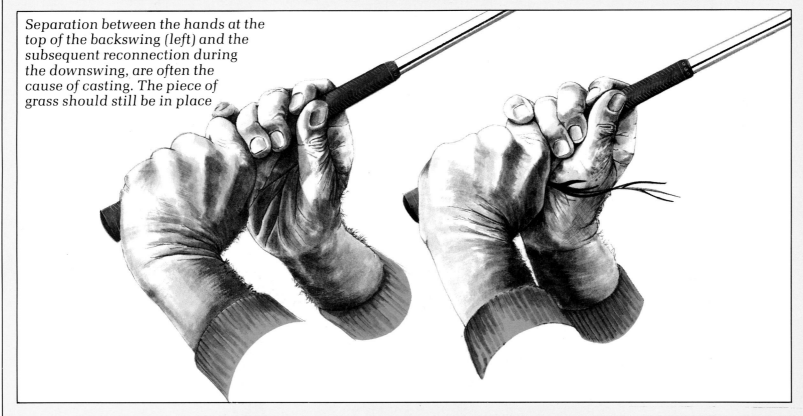

Separation between the hands at the top of the backswing (left) and the subsequent reconnection during the downswing, are often the cause of casting. The piece of grass should still be in place

Make sure you clear your left hip around to the left during your downswing

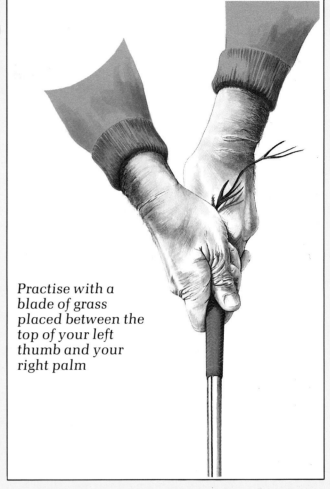

Practise with a blade of grass placed between the top of your left thumb and your right palm

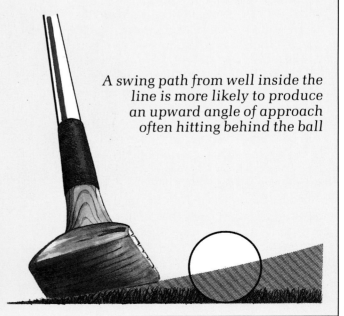

A swing path from well inside the line is more likely to produce an upward angle of approach often hitting behind the ball

Cure your smother and get that ball up

We have all experienced at some time or other, a round of golf when it has seemed almost impossible to get the ball to rise much above ground level. This holds especially true when using the fairway woods and long irons, and you can even find a 7-iron shot flying no higher than a normal 2-iron.

Even with the ball teed up it becomes impossible to attain the hoped-for elevation, and the only time the shot looks right is when driving from an unusually elevated teeing ground.

The more you try to get the ball airborne, the more it hugs the grass. The villain of this particular frustration is the action that produces smothering. The smother is, in fact, related to the hook and has the effect of making the ball stay very low, usually turning to the left.

This kind of poor shot is the direct result of the clubface being hooded at the moment it strikes the ball. The loft built into the club at manufacture has been almost eliminated and it is possible, when using the more powerful clubs, for the loft to be actually reversed. The player has turned the clubface over at impact which makes it impossible, therefore, to hit the ball into the air. In fact, if it was possible, the ball would travel underground.

Now there are various degrees of smothering depending upon how much the clubface is turned over at impact. Should the loft on the club be altered only slightly, then the result is a low-flying ball that will travel, at maximum, only about two-thirds of the normal distance through the air.

We know that it is a hooded face at impact that causes the smother, but what causes the hooded clubface?

There are four main reasons:
1 A poor grip.
2 An incorrect position at the top of the backswing even though the grip may be correct.
3 A lateral sway to the left with the hands in front of the ball.
4 Hooding the face at impact combined with rolling shoulders (producing a smothered pull).

Any one of these four will cause the right hand and arm to overpower the left during the downswing, so turning the clubface over to give a hooded result. To find a remedy, start with the grip, which is the main culprit in smothering. Make sure that the right hand is not round and under the shaft in an over-powerful position. If it is, then it will dominate the left hand and turn the clubface over at impact. Or it could be at address that the left hand is positioned too far over to the right showing three-and-a-half to four

Gary Player holds the clubface square through the shot to avoid a smother

Cocking the wrists too quickly(1) leads to a steep outside backswing, minimal shoulder turn and a piccolo grip with the left wrist under the shaft(2). The downswing starts by throwing the clubhead, as the left hand closes on the shaft(3). To avoid smothering always start the backswing by keeping the clubhead close to the turf(4)

knuckles.

If this is the case, you are in real trouble because this will cause the clubface to close at the top of the backswing. As a result, it will be closed at impact and then a smothered shot will be produced.

You will have to move both hands round to the left until the inverted 'V's formed by the first finger and thumb of each hand appear to you, as you look down (from the bird's eye view), to be pointing up the middle of the shaft. To the onlooker they will appear to be pointing between the player's right shoulder and neck.

At first the alteration in the grip will feel very unnatural, but with diligent practice it will soon become commonplace. With this grip, the hands will not turn the clubface to a closed position at the top of the backswing nor at impact. If, however, the hands have not been altered sufficiently to the position just described, you may get a hook and that is the best you can expect.

A second cause of smothering is a closed clubface at the top of the backswing. This can still be obtained even using a correct grip and is generally caused by rolling the clubface anti-clockwise during the swing. Should the player fail to compensate for the faulty movement by not rolling the clubface clockwise on the way back to the ball, it will be hooded at impact.

To check this point, make sure the right wrist, not the left, is under the shaft at the top of the backswing. Do not just swing back and stop to check if your right wrist is in the correct position. It can be done only by an observer, so ask a friend to look for you. Better still, seek the help of your club professional. A half-closed clubface at the top of the swing is what you are seeking ideally.

There is one more fault worth mentioning and that is try not to have a loose left hand at the top of the backswing. When this happens the left wrist is under the shaft. The left hand bends back and opens. This is called a piccolo grip.

When this fault occurs the player

Cure your smother and get that ball up

starts his downswing by shutting the left hand forcibly, which results in a 'throw' of the clubhead and causes hitting from the top. The clubface closes, and if it closes to the point of being hooded, then the result is a smothered shot. So keep the left-hand grip firm during the swing ... but not to the point of being rigid.

Reason number three does not really apply to the driver but does apply with all the other clubs. It is smothering caused by swaying towards the target. Why not so much with the driver? Simply because the ball is teed up and a hooded face in this instance may cause the ball to be struck above the clubface on the paintwork – a weak, high shot will always be the result.

This kind of action is always caused by not releasing the clubhead in the impact area – mainly due to a stiff-wristed action. The player instinctively knows he has to get the clubhead to the ball, but due to his wooden-like action has to sway to the left to make contact. This can also, to some extent, cause the right shoulder to turn too soon. This brings his hands in front of the clubhead at impact with the face hooded and the natural loft diminished.

You can test this for yourself. Stand at an address position and move laterally to the left leaving the clubhead behind the ball. By doing so you will see what is meant. The loft will start to disappear. If this swaying action should be your fault, it is quite easy to rectify by keeping your head behind the ball throughout the backswing and downswing until after impact. This will make you release the club-

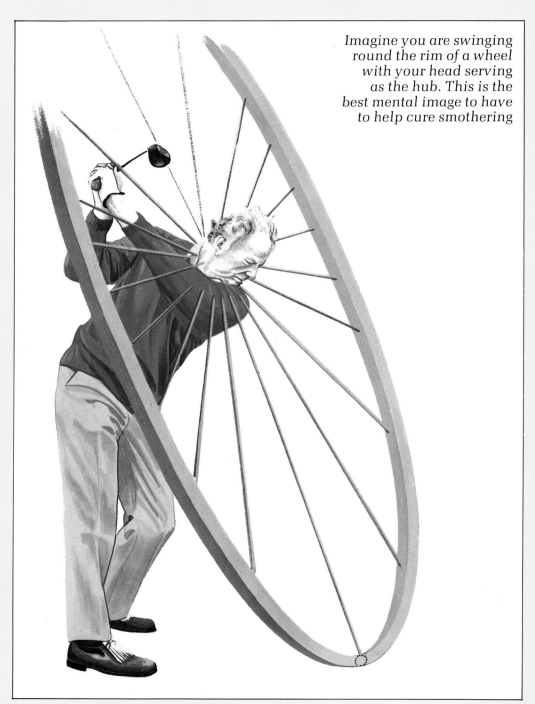

Imagine you are swinging round the rim of a wheel with your head serving as the hub. This is the best mental image to have to help cure smothering

An incorrect grip is the main cause of smothering. Too strong a grip, ie, four knuckles of the left hand showing, will cause the clubface to be closed at impact

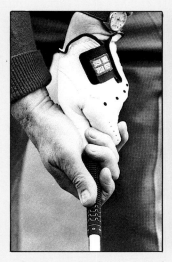

A correct grip should only show one and a half knuckles of the left hand. The back of the left hand should face the target

head through the shot.

Cause number four is the natural one affecting mainly the beginner. It takes place in a swing that is radically wrong from the start, and goes hand-in-hand with a pull-type action.

It happens when a backswing is too steep, so making the downswing outside the line of flight. (This can also cause a slice, but in this instance you are only considering the smother.)

Likewise, it can happen when the backswing is correct but the player, at the start of the downswing, throws the clubhead out and forwards. The right shoulder reacts in response to this movement by rolling round and the clubface becomes hooded with diminished loft at impact.

The cure for the steep backswing is similar to the pull and slice. Assuming that your grip, stance, alignment and posture are correct, make sure that as soon as the backswing commences the clubhead is then made to swing around on an inclined plane, then stay on the path the clubhead started on.

This will give you a correct position at the top of the backswing from which you can deliver the clubhead to the ball on the correct line with every chance of the clubface presenting its true loft at impact.

It is possible that a correct top of the backswing movement can go wrong if the clubhead is thrown out at the very commencement of the downswing.

Should this be your trouble, then make the clubhead swing back to the ball feeling it is going to travel on a path near to your right toe and away from your left as it swings through: in other words, from inside-to-out. This is an over-correction which will more often than not produce a swing track through the ball going from inside-to-straight.

Finally, it is worth checking on ball position in relation to feet at address. If the ball is too far to the right for the particular club being used, then some of the loft is taken off the clubface.

However, many a good player will want to use this ball position when playing into a very strong wind and hoping to produce a low flying, wind-avoiding shot.

Corrections for smothering:

1 Check your grip, so the inverted 'V's are in their correct place.
2 Have the position of the wrists at the top of the backswing checked. The right wrist, not the left, must be under the shaft.
3 Make sure there is no lateral sway to the left by keeping the head behind the ball until after impact.
4 Check that you start the backswing correctly, and once that is achieved make sure the swing back to the ball is moving on an in-to-out path.

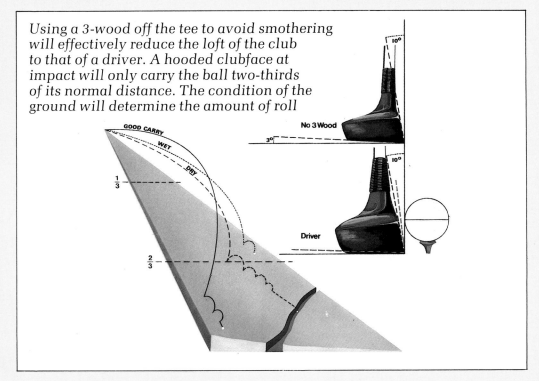

Using a 3-wood off the tee to avoid smothering will effectively reduce the loft of the club to that of a driver. A hooded clubface at impact will only carry the ball two-thirds of its normal distance. The condition of the ground will determine the amount of roll

The myth of the late hit

Advice about late hitting is the enemy of many golfers and the myth of this particular swing position is based on 'frozen' action pictures of the game's great players. Usually, the description accompanying such pictures points out how the player has kept his wrists fully cocked, as an aid to increased power and accuracy, when his hands are waist-high on the downswing. Most golfers who see these pictures assume that this must be an ideal position and set out to reproduce it. However, there is no such thing as late hitting in the first-class player – and assuredly there is no such thing for the handicap player.

What the camera does not show is that the top player's clubhead, at the so-called late hitting position, is catching up the hands all the time so that by the time the ball is reached, both hands and clubhead are together. Any golfer trying to copy the late hitting position has no chance of getting the clubhead to the ball in time. The hands will have gone past the ball before the clubhead can catch up and, at impact, the clubface will be open. The likely result is either a slice or a pull-slice or, if an in-to-out swing path has been maintained, a push or push slice can be expected.

The average golfer should be thinking about the opposite to a late hit and concentrate on getting the clubhead in sooner. Jack Nicklaus himself has said that you cannot get the clubhead to the ball soon enough when seeking power and accuracy. So what is meant by the advice to get the clubhead in sooner? It means that the clubhead must be made to reach the ball just before the shoulders have

returned parallel to the intended line of flight. Do not confuse this with the fault of hitting too early. This occurs when the player throws the clubhead out and around from the top of the backswing, not unlike casting a line when fishing. There is no doubt that 'frozen' action pictures produced by the high-speed camera are responsible for putting more golfers on the wrong path to the late hit than almost any other factor.

The player who copies the late hitting position lacks distance with shots because there is no clubhead speed at impact. When wrist action is deliberately delayed through impact, maximum clubhead speed occurs a long while after the ball has been struck. Many golfers slice as a result and then try to hit even later when seeking a cure. This only aggravates the fault. If you concentrate on hitting late then you will be too late. Let the

The so-called 'late hitting position'. Do not try to copy this position but understand the powers that produce it

Holding the clubhead back causes the shoulders to turn too soon leaving the hands ahead of the clubhead and resulting in either a straight pull left or a slice

natural forces look after themselves and do not try to manufacture them by conscious effort. For a practical test, go to the practice area and hit some shots, deliberately keeping your wrists fully cocked on the downswing. The type of poor shots already mentioned will be produced.

Why then are the wrists seen to be fully cocked at waist height on the downswing? After all, the camera does not lie. It happens because with good players the wrists do not cock to their maximum until they are on their way back to the ball and a subconscious flail-type action is produced. This flail action brings the

By trying to get the clubhead to the ball 'sooner', the clubhead travels at high speed to reach impact simultaneously with the hands

player's hands automatically waist-high on the downswing with the wrists fully cocked. It is this effect, frozen by the camera, that gives the illusion of deliberately hitting late.

In a proper swing this simply happens and does *not* have to be consciously produced. As for the flail, this arises from a change of direction – from the clubhead going back to starting down. Add to this the weight of the clubhead, which during the swing is measured in pounds rather

Getting the clubhead to the ball at the same time as the hands and before the shoulders have turned provides power and accuracy

than ounces, and its speed and you are generating a force of up to a ton at impact. The result of these forces is so great that the wrists will break to their maximum on the way back to the ball in the downswing.

Top players know that they must move the clubhead at lightning speed from the waist-high position so that by the time the hands return back to the ball, the clubhead will have travelled the greater part of its arc and pass the hands at impact. The truth is that this is unlikely to happen and the real effect is for the clubhead to arrive at the ball at the same time as the hands. Therefore, the feeling for which you need to strive is that the clubhead is going to arrive at the ball first. The moral is to forget late hitting (delayed action) and concentrate instead on getting the clubhead back in time along the correct swing path and then you will have the clubface square coupled with maximum speed where it matters most – at impact.

The shoulders and hands have hardly moved but the clubhead is catching up as impact draws nearer

Groove your swing to eradicate the pull

A pulled shot is one that travels in a straight line to the left of the intended target. If you hit a shot that starts out to the left but then curls further left towards the end of flight, then that is a pulled hook. Both these shots occur as a result of an outside-to-in swing path which is why the pull is from the same stable as the slice. However, whereas the slice involves an out-to-in swing path with an open clubface at impact, the pull involves the same swing path but with the clubface square at impact to that swing path line. If the clubface is closed at impact along that swing path then a pulled hook will result.

The first thing to be done when faced with a pull is to stop swinging the clubhead across the line of intended flight. Start by checking the basics: grip, stance, ball position and alignment. When these are in order, the next most important factor is the first movement of the backswing. You should be starting the backswing all in one piece – that is, shoulders, arms, hands and clubhead dominated by the left side around a fixed axis. This makes sure that the clubhead starts back naturally inside the intended line of flight for about the first twelve inches of the swing. Usually from such a start the rest of the backswing will follow to a good position at the top, from where the downswing can be delivered in the correct form.

With an incorrect swing, the one travelling from outside-to-in, the club has been started back on an outside line from where it is impossible to reach the top of the swing in a correct position. If the swing starts outside, then it invariably stays outside and returns to the ball on an out-to-in path. Then the right shoulder moves round in response instead of under, and this, in turn, produces a flat follow-through. Therefore, it is vital to start the swing in one piece as this sets the swing path on the inside.

Although you may start the swing on the inside and reach a correct position at the top, it is still possible to pull the shot by throwing the clubhead outside the line with the initial movement of the downswing. This occurs mainly when the player is striving for extra distance. This action makes the right shoulder turn outwards instead of under the chin.

Assuming that you have reached the correct position at the top, the correct start to the downswing makes the hips and shoulders start to turn towards their position at address. The weight wants to move on to the left foot with the wrists automatically maintaining their hinged position to about waist-level on the downswing.

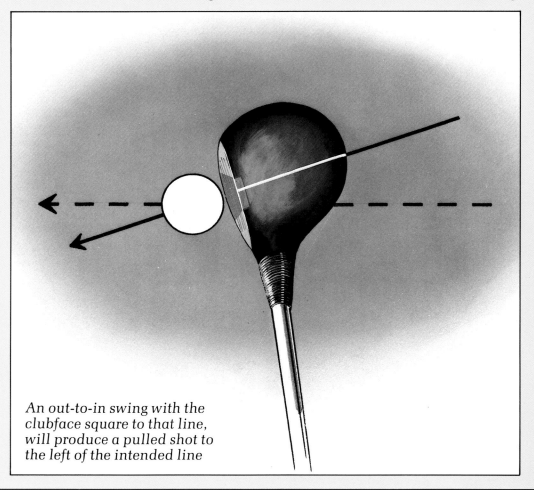

An out-to-in swing with the clubface square to that line, will produce a pulled shot to the left of the intended line

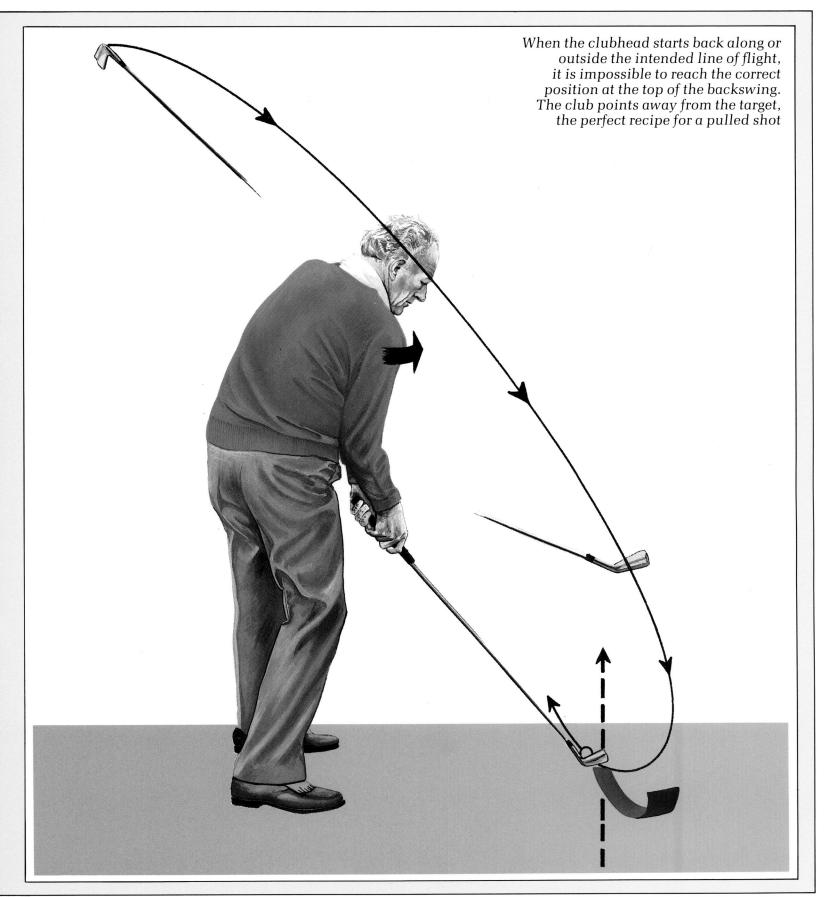

When the clubhead starts back along or outside the intended line of flight, it is impossible to reach the correct position at the top of the backswing. The club points away from the target, the perfect recipe for a pulled shot

Groove your swing to eradicate the pull

As the downswing continues the club gathers speed, and it should have reached maximum speed by the time that impact is achieved, on line, swinging towards the target or even a little to the right of it. The main point is that once you reach the correct position halfway in the downswing then it is impossible to hit the ball from outside-to-in – you have to hit from the inside.

One other point to remember is to position the ball at address inside the left heel. If the ball is too far forward in the stance, either opposite or outside the left toe, then the clubhead will reach the ball as the swing path travels back inside the target line and a pull will result.

However, no matter how long you play, there will be occasions when you succumb to the impulse to apply more power than you can control. Such extra effort will be applied through leverage and forced 'force', which will result in inaccuracy and loss of control. When you are in control of the club during the swing, you can sense what is happening throughout the action of the swing. That makes it possible for the clubface to meet the ball correctly at the moment of impact.

An exaggerated inside takeaway(1) will place the player in an incorrect position at the top of the swing and the downswing will commence with the shoulders throwing the clubhead outside the line and across the ball after impact(2)

1

2

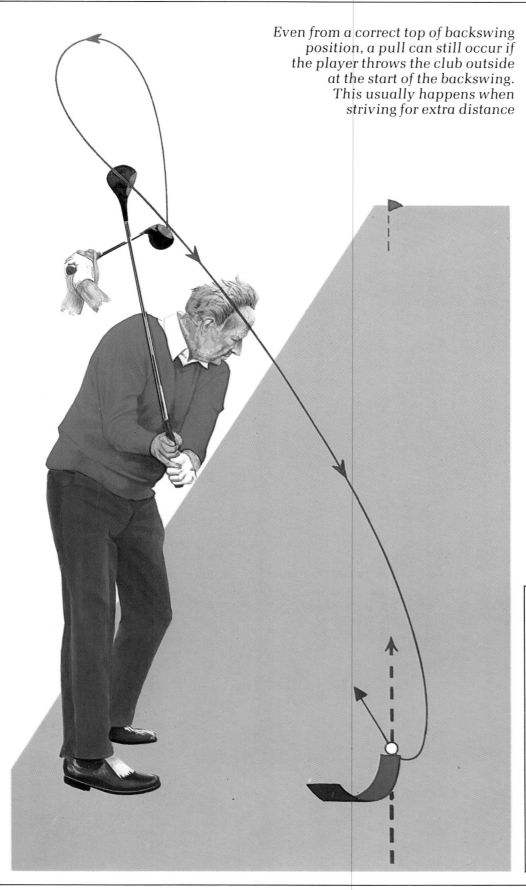

Even from a correct top of backswing position, a pull can still occur if the player throws the club outside at the start of the backswing. This usually happens when striving for extra distance

Corrections for pulling

1 Check your outside-in swing. If you pull shots consistently you must be striking the ball from the outside.

2 Check the basics – grip, stance, alignment to target, and ball position – when at address.

3 Check your start to the backswing. The left shoulder, arms, and club-head must start together.

4 Check the top of the backswing. The clubshaft must be parallel to the target line.

5 Check the start of the downswing. The clubhead must be kept inside the intended line of flight.

6 Check that you are swinging the clubhead and not using 'forced' force.

Simple ways to avoid an overswing

Many golfers tend to be worried about swinging the club back too far. Very often the club travels beyond the horizontal at the top of the backswing so that a certain degree of control is lost. Often this occurs because the left arm is allowed to bend during the backswing but it may also arise through an opening up of the left hand at the top of the backswing. For the golfer who has one or other of these faults the problem may not be easy to correct, but it is obvious why the problem arises.

However, there is another cause of an overswing which is often less simple to spot. In this type of case the player may swing up to the top of the backswing with what looks to be a fairly good swing and yet the wrists somehow allow the club to drop beyond the horizontal. What causes this is that the player is trying for 'width' in the backswing. There is often a tendency among club golfers to try to produce almost too wide a swing so that both arms are kept fairly straight in the backswing and the

wristcock is delayed. When you see a player like Nicklaus doing this, what you must remember is that he has exceptionally strong hands and wrists and is able to get into a virtually orthodox position at the top of the backswing. However, for the woman golfer who tends to delay the wristcock in the backswing it is often impossible to cock the wrists quickly enough to prepare for the downswing without allowing the club to go beyond the horizontal.

The cause of this tendency to cock

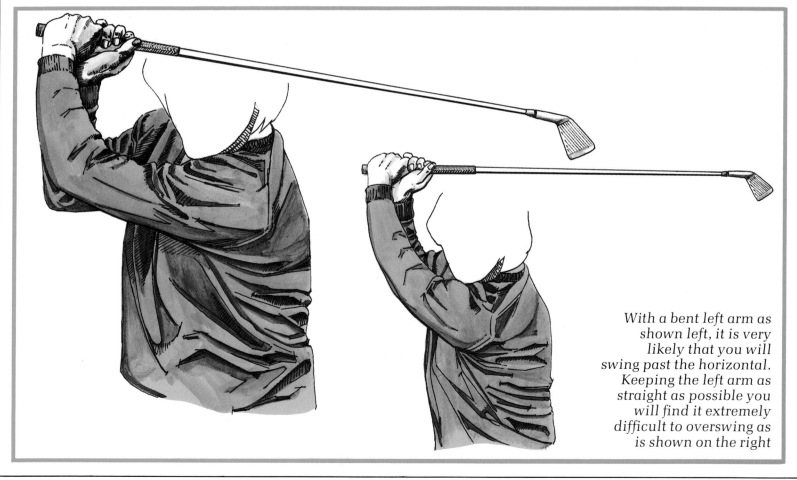

With a bent left arm as shown left, it is very likely that you will swing past the horizontal. Keeping the left arm as straight as possible you will find it extremely difficult to overswing as is shown on the right

1

2

3

4

5

6

7

8

On this wedge shot, Ben Crenshaw retains control despite his long back-swing. Starting the backswing(1) and there is an immediate impression of the width of arc he is trying to create as the club continues upwards(2). At the top(3) he has achieved a full shoulder turn but the club is well short of the horizontal and he is poised to thrust off his right side while maintaining the angle between his arms and the shaft(4). Approaching impact and the hands are beginning to release the clubhead(5) and eventually square it up(6). Just after impact and the width of arc created in the back-swing is reflected by this position(7), his momentum carrying him on

Simple ways to avoid an overswing

the wrists late is one of looking at top-class golfers and trying to mimic them, or perhaps even looking at pictures in golf books or magazines and trying to copy these. When you look at a good golfer making a backswing, he often gives the impression that the hands and wrists are not working until about halfway up the backswing.

What you should realize is that for most good golfers the hands and wrists are really active as soon as the club moves away from address. The hands and wrists are usually beginning to cock right from the moment of the takeaway but because the arms are also moving no wristcock shows until the clubhead is perhaps hip-height in the backswing. Particularly with the iron shots, the professional golfer is almost always conscious of hand action right from the start of the swing. However, this may not be apparent to the spectator. Frequently the club player has an idea that the wrists should not work until halfway up the backswing and, therefore, delays the wristcock almost too late. By the time the hands and wrists do begin to work the arms are often almost to the top of the backswing so that the wristcock simply produces this unsatisfactory overswing together with loss of control.

The main problems that tend to arise from an overswing are loss of length and power and also possible problems of striking the ground behind the ball, particularly with the longer irons.

The best exercise for the golfer who has this problem of tending to overswing, is to practise hitting a few

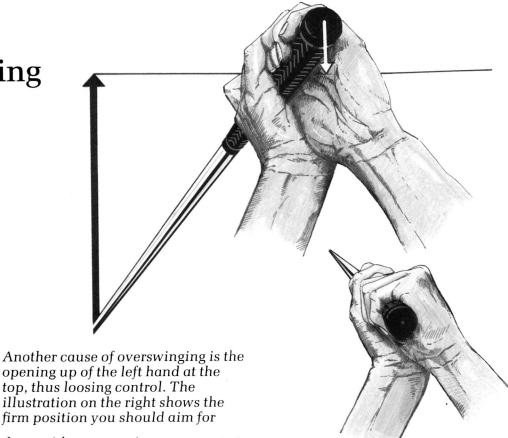

Another cause of overswinging is the opening up of the left hand at the top, thus loosing control. The illustration on the right shows the firm position you should aim for

shots with a 6- or 7-iron, concentrating on breaking the wrists very early in the takeaway. The earlier you are able to use the hands in the backswing the sooner you are prepared with the necessary power to change direction and make a swing through the ball. For this reason, players who tend to pick the club up sharply will often have a noticeably short swing. Obviously you can go to extremes where the hands appear to work almost too early, giving the impression of an unsuitably steep backswing. The problem here is very often not that the hands work too early or indeed do too much, but simply that the arms are not moving sufficiently. Clearly if you cock the wrists almost immediately the club is taken away without moving the arms, and will give the impression of cocking the wrists too soon. If, on the other hand,

you simply move the arms away at the same time this would produce the correct action.

So, if you are troubled with an over-lengthy swing, tending to hit heavy shots with the long irons or feeling some loss of power, try to work on the idea of using the hands and wrists rather earlier in the backswing thus setting yourself up for a powerful downswing.

Bear in mind, however, that the clubhead must always stay reasonably low to the ground in the first inches of the takeaway – moving inside the target line – and not being picked up too steeply. Active hand action in the takeaway should not be equated to a steep takeaway. The clubhead can still move on a shallow arc and yet set the hands and wrists up for a powerful attack on the ball.

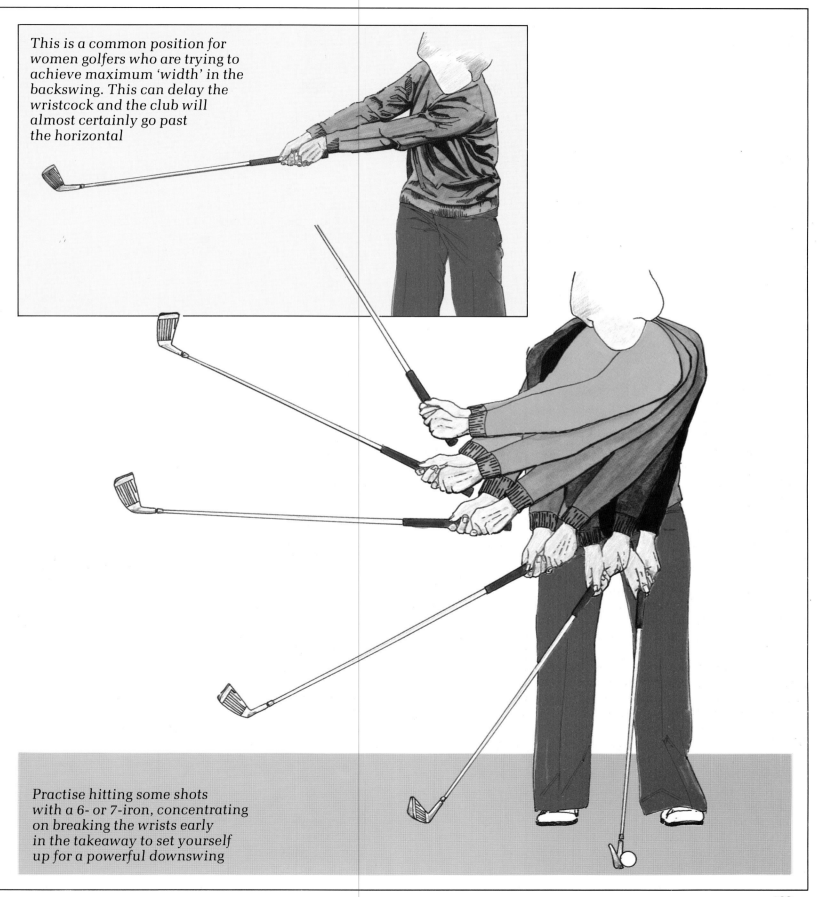

This is a common position for women golfers who are trying to achieve maximum 'width' in the backswing. This can delay the wristcock and the club will almost certainly go past the horizontal

Practise hitting some shots with a 6- or 7-iron, concentrating on breaking the wrists early in the takeaway to set yourself up for a powerful downswing

Curing the shank

Ashank is probably the most destructive and mentally devastating shot in golf for it strikes without warning and invariably sends the ball into an irretrievable spot. There is, however, a very simple cure which, with a little perseverance and use of a practical exercise, should quickly be of help if you have this problem. The position of the ball in golf, on the ground and to the side of you, determines two major factors:

1 The fact that the ball is on the ground means that the club must swing up and down.

2 Because the ball is to the side of you, at the same time that the club swings up and down, it should be on an arc that approaches the ball from the inside, hits straight through and returns to the inside. The backswing should position the club correctly, which takes in two elements: plane and direction. When the club is swung on too flat a plane with the arc too far behind you, it will swing too far away from you on the downswing, thus hitting the ball in the heel of the club with a wooden club and on the shank with an iron. The natural reaction is for the player to stand further away from the ball which in itself creates an even flatter arc and makes things even worse.

Most players with a tendency to shank are not aware that the backswing is made to position the club. They have usually concentrated solely on the pivot on the backswing. If you only pivot and allow the club to associate itself too closely with the pivot, the backswing ends with the club travelling backwards instead of upwards and therefore swings for-wards instead of down in the downswing. The inter-relationship between the clubface and swing arc is such that when the arc becomes too flat, the clubface rolls open far too rapidly during the backswing, and then closes much too quickly on the throughswing.

There are two exercises that can greatly assist anyone with this problem. You are trying to turn the shoulders correctly but at the same time swing the club up so that it finishes the backswing parallel to the

Hitting practice shots with your backside close to a wall will eliminate a flat swing plane

ball-target line. To stop the club swinging too far behind in the backswing, practice should be done with something in the way of the wrong movement, such as a soft, high hedge. With this obstruction in the way, as the shoulders turn the club is forced on the correct upward arc. Initially the hedge will take something of a beating no doubt but in a fairly short time the desired effect can be achieved and you will improve.

Practising on a slope with the ball below the feet is also helpful. In this situation it is virtually impossible to pivot very much, added to which the downward view of the ball gives you the desired picture of the necessity of swinging the club up and down as opposed to round the body. The feeling needs to be one of swinging the hands, arms and club high enough in the backswing to reach the bottom of the ball, which should be positioned distinctly below the feet.

Both these exercises are most useful for those players who tend to swing the club on too flat an arc, irrespective of whether this actually creates a shank. A flat swing almost always starts from a much too open-shouldered address position. You are trying, remember, to swing the club up on the inside, but an open shoulder situation leads to too much effort being made to get the club inside, hence a flat arc. If you suffer with a flat swing your feeling should be one of having the arc inside by addressing the ball with the shoulders closed, and thus the concentration can be on the hand and arm action. Swing the club up and down on this predetermined inside arc.

Playing the ball too far forward at address aligns the shoulders too far to the left

From this position the arms must move around the body on a plane that is too flat

Chapter 6 IMPROVING YOUR GAME

Golf is a game where there is always room for improvement. During the course of a round, a golfer is faced with many different types of shot that may require special techniques. Knowing how to handle these various shots can bring immediate improvement to your score. This chapter tells you when and how to shape your shots, how to combat uneven and poor lies, how to get out of trouble and how to utilize your time on the practice ground to the very best effect. As your golf becomes more advanced you will be able to apply these various techniques during the course of an actual game.

When and how to shape your shots

Golf being a game of ball control, it is imperative to accept that what the ball does is totally dependent upon what the clubhead is doing at impact. The clubface can be square, open or closed at impact but it can also be strong (de-lofted) or weak. The swing path can be straight through, out-to-in or in-to-out. Additionally, the club can either be hitting down, up or through (parallel to the ground).

This shows clearly that there are many combinations of the clubface, swing path and angle of approach which will flight the ball in different ways. A particular type of contact may be useful or not depending on the situation. Club selection is also most important since clubs with different lofts will shape the ball differently even with exactly the same conditions at impact.

All things being equal, curving shots in either direction is possible with the straight-faced clubs since the contact is high enough up the back of the ball to apply side-spin. However, it is usually easier to play long shots left to right since right-to-left shots call for a closed clubface, and with straight-faced clubs there is the obvious difficulty of getting the ball in the air. A right-to-left shot also requires a good lie because the necessary in-to-out swing path is particularly shallow.

When trying to play a fade round a right-hand dog-leg, tee the ball lower than normal. The lower tee will cause you to hit down slightly making it easier to hit a controlled fade. Swing slightly out-to-in. Use a driver or a 1-iron as it is easier to hit a fade with a straight-faced club

Conversely, short shots are very difficult to bend left to right since the extra loft and open clubface creates backspin as opposed to side-spin. In normal circumstances then, if for some reason you need to shape shots, it is much easier to fade long shots (straight-faced clubs) and draw short shots (the lofted clubs).

The lie of the ball has a specific bearing on what type of shot is easiest. A tight lie requires a steep swing to create a solid impact. This type of action encourages an open clubface at impact and therefore a fade is the right shot to picture from this type of lie. Conversely, when the ball is sitting up in soft grass this encourages a sweeping action which tends to close the clubface and therefore a draw is the natural shape shot.

Sloping lies produce automatic impact conditions. When the ball is below the feet, the club is bound to swing on a more upright arc which tends to create an open clubface at impact, so a fade should be allowed for. When the ball is above the feet, a shallower in-to-in hitting area closes the club so this time allow for a draw.

How to play dog-legs
In playing dog-legs, those holes that bend to the right from the tee are best approached with the ball teed somewhat lower than normal for the driver. The lower tee will automatically create a slight downward blow, and the straightness of the clubface making contact on the back of the ball makes it easy to fade. Holes that bend to the left and call for a draw are often best tackled by using a lofted wood. A draw requires the clubface to be closed at impact. With the driver you have very little margin for error and unless your natural shot is a draw with a driver it is always far easier and much safer to play this shot with the 3-wood.

Playing in crosswinds really can test all of us. In a right-to-left wind with shots to the green, over-club and swing easily. This will tend to leave the clubface open and therefore counteract the wind. In a left-to-right

When trying for a draw around a left-hand dog-leg, tee the ball higher than for a fade and use a lofted wood, not the driver. It is easier and safer than the driver which has very little room for error. To get the draw the clubface must be closed slightly at impact. Swing in-to-out

wind it is often better to under-club and hit hard which will tend to close the clubface at impact, again counteracting the wind. Tee shots in a crosswind for the most part should simply be set off on the windward side allowing for the wind to bring the ball back. This way the wind is being used to attain distance as opposed to those shots to the green when the wind is deliberately counteracted in order for the ball to stop.

While all the above is true, most of us have our own favourite shot

in which we have confidence. However, this advice should help you not to play the wrong shot at the wrong time. Therefore remember the following:
1 The straighter the club the easier to fade.
2 Do not attempt to draw the driver unless you do it naturally.
3 When the lie is tight, play a fade.
4 Do not attempt to draw the ball unless the lie is good.
5 Do not attempt to fade the short irons.

How to combat uneven lies

Do you ever stop and ponder why you mishit the last shot? Was it through a bad swing, some distraction or was it because you were playing from an uneven lie and did not have the experience through lack of practice from a similar situation?

You see it every day: whenever golfers go out to practise, the first thing they do is find some even piece of turf. Who can blame them? After all, they have gone there to correct some fault, to practise to maintain standards, or play better shots, and we all get our best results hitting shots from ideal lies.

There is no doubt about it that striking the ball from level ground is sensible and a help towards producing a good swing. However, the hard facts are that you can only be sure during a round of having eighteen good even lies on the tees from which you will be playing.

Have you ever stopped to consider how many times during a round of golf you will encounter a flat fairway lie? A low-handicap man, who will be playing fewer shots anyway than the high handicapper, will not have more than, on average, one-third of his fairway shots from even lies – at most, six or seven shots per round. Yet nearly every golfer seems to overlook the fact that so much of his golf will be from less-than-perfect positions.

In general terms, during play, no conscious notice is registered when negotiating slight slopes or undulations – one foot an inch or so above the other and so on. Nature will compensate automatically and make adjustments.

Carry out the following test for yourself. Set yourself up to play a shot with an open stance – left foot up to four inches back from the right foot – with your shoulders parallel to the intended line of flight. Once at that address position, and after a 'waggle' or two to get really relaxed, stop for a moment and then look down at your knees.

Although your feet are in an open position, the knees are likely to be parallel to the intended line of flight. Your left leg will be bent a little more than the right leg. All this happened because nature dictated the correct posture and balance.

The same holds true when adopting a shut stance – right foot back from the left foot – with the shoulders square to target line. This time, of course, it will be the right leg that is bent more than the left leg, but the knees remain parallel to the intended line of flight.

These responsive movements can be compared with what happens when you walk up a hill. Without acting consciously you lean forwards to maintain balance – to centralize your centre of gravity but walking downhill you tend to lean backwards.

Here is another example: when walking along a hillslope you lean towards the hill. With the slope going from left to right your right leg will be quite straight and your left leg will be partly bent. Obviously the reverse happens when walking in the other direction. Now, if these things can happen instinctively during everyday life, why do we golfers make such a fuss about uphill, downhill and across lies? And why practise continually from level land when so many

When playing from an uneven lie with shoulders square to the target, your knees will follow suit regardless of your stance

uneven shots are bound to be in demand in a normal game?

It is sensible during your practice sessions to spend a little time – do not overdo it because it could alter your swing permanently – learning how best to play from awkward lies. You will also get experience of how the flight of the ball is affected.

Most slopes during play go unnoticed but there are some that are quite severe. Many of these are experienced while playing on seaside courses, when quite often we get more than our fair share. Links courses, like St Andrews and Royal

When playing awkward shots natural balance will set your knees parallel to the line of the shoulders, at address and impact

When playing from an uphill lie, try to make the clubhead follow the line of the slope at the start of the backswing and through the impact area

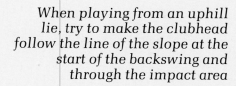

St George's in Great Britain, readily come to mind.

For those who like to have detail in their mind when tackling *exaggerated* uneven lies here is some advice about playing the ball on five different types of slope. Before going into such detail there is one thing that applies to all of them and this is the most important thing. The natural posture adopted when negotiating a shot from a slope will dictate the shape of your swing. Do not fight the sort of swing that your stance will produce. You are going to get a certain shaped shot from different lies — whether it be a slice or a hook — and you should learn to recognize this.

If circumstances dictate that you are likely to slice, or hook, play a high or low flying ball, then do not try to adapt your swing to neutralize the prospect. Far better to acknowledge the likely flight that can be expected and allow for it.

It is important, too, when playing from a noticeable slope, to accept the fact that your length of swing — back and through — and the distance achieved will be curtailed somewhat, the amount naturally depending on the severity of the undulation.

The uphill shot

We shall start with the uphill shot with the ball already at rest on the slope. Nature will tell you to have your right leg straight and your left knee bent. The weight will be mainly on the right foot, and the right shoulder much lower than usual. The ball will be positioned, in general terms, midway between the left foot and the middle of stance.

From such a stance you will be hitting the ball more on the upswing causing it to fly higher than usual. This means that the ball will not travel as far as when playing from level ground. Nature is turning, say, a 5-iron into a 6-, 7- or even an 8-iron.

So if the uphill distance should indicate a 5-iron then take out of the bag a 4- or 3-iron. On occasions a 4-wood held down the grip could be the answer to your problem.

Take into consideration, too, that because your left leg is bent more than usual due to the slope it will restrict the length of both the back and the through swing. The thing you need to concentrate on during your swing is trying to make the clubhead follow the line of the slope — the result being that, for iron or wood shots, you will be making (naturally within limits) a normal backswing.

Through the impact area you do not want to dig the clubface into the ground, and the answer is to keep the clubhead moving up the line of the slope. The danger is that as the weight is so much on the right foot to neutralize the slope, the player can lose his balance easily during the swing causing him either to lean or fall back. Watch out for this trap and try to keep as steady as possible throughout the action.

It is common to pull this shot to the left so allow for it and aim off to the right. How much you aim off target is governed by the severity of slope.

The downhill shot

Downhill lie problems are reversed

How to combat uneven lies

and the main weight is now on the left leg, with the right knee bent more than is customary. The best position for the ball during this shot is from the centre of the stance to around half way back towards the right foot. Such generalization depends largely on the individual and steepness of the slope. It moves the bottom part of the swing arc back into this area.

You will get a steeper backswing and once again on returning to the ball make the clubhead follow the line of the slope as much as possible.

From downhill lies you will experience a lower flying shot so now you can drop down a club or two. If a 6-iron would seem correct then take out a 7-iron, and so forth.

The biggest danger is topping. This is due to the natural reaction to sway down the slope just before impact. Even playing correctly on a downhill lie you may experience a slight fade or even a slice, so it will not hurt to make some adjustment and aim a little to the left.

Standing below the ball

Now for standing below the ball – the first of the cross slopes – with the ball above the level of your feet. To stop you standing too upright, hold the club a little lower down the grip. Position yourself to the ball so that it is more or less central at address. The weight will be divided between both feet but automatically back towards the heels.

The swing plane will be flatter than usual and the tendency will be to draw or hook the ball to the left. So anticipate it and set yourself up at address aiming a little right of target.

More often than not, this allowance pays off. Keeping your hands slightly ahead of the clubface during the swing will help you to minimize the expected draw.

As you will be holding the club somewhat down the shaft, distance will be reduced, and to compensate it will be necessary to use one or two clubs stronger than otherwise.

Standing above the ball

When standing above the ball you face a more difficult shot because as you are standing above the level of the ball you may feel that you are going to topple forward on to it when you are swinging.

Position the ball opposite a midway point between the feet, and as you will have to reach for the ball you must stand a shade closer than routine. It also helps to bend the knees more than normal. Hold the club at full length and have the hands just a bit in front of the ball at address with the weight back towards the heels. A fade or slice is in prospect so you will find it helpful to close the clubface a little but make sure you do this before taking up your grip.

Nature will insist that your backswing becomes more upright than it was before, and your backswing (and the throughswing) will definitely be restricted – do not fight this. Accept the fact that you will lose distance and use a more powerful club than perhaps you might think you need.

To offset that expected slice or fade, aim somewhat to the left. The amount of slice can vary quite a lot. The slice happens because it is difficult to hit straight through the ball and it is far

easier, unfortunately, due to the awkward stance, to swing the clubhead on a track from out-to-in across the target line.

Combined downhill and side slopes

This is a difficult one when you find a downhill lie coupled with the ball being below the feet. Socketing is not uncommon from this situation. The reason for this is that anxiety creeps in and makes most golfers tense up and grip too tightly. When this happens, free swinging is exchanged for a stiff-like action and the player sways forwards and sideways along the ground slope. The clubhead is then pushed right into the ball – hence causing the shank.

At address, have the ball positioned just right of centre. As the weight will fall mainly on the left foot, so the left leg will be straightish and the right knee bent. You will find the weight also moving towards your toes. Because it is partly a downhill lie you will achieve more distance than usual so select a club less powerful than otherwise required.

You do not want to swing too upright so keep the clubhead low to the ground as far as possible on the backswing and throughswing. Put another way, try to keep the clubhead following the slope of the ground.

There you have the most common of the awkward lies and how best to combat them, and remember, as explained, that the ball is more than likely to travel off line. Accept that fact and do not attempt to change your swing in the hope of hitting straight on target – far better to make allowances while lining up.

1

2

When playing from a downhill lie(1), your weight will be on the left foot. The right leg will have to be bent more to compensate. Position the ball further back in the stance with hands ahead of the ball

When playing a shot from above the level of your feet(2) you can expect a flatter backswing. This will cause a draw or hook so allow for this by aiming right of the target at address

3

4

When above the ball(3) stand closer than usual with the ball centred in the stance. You will have a more upright backswing than normal from which you will fade the ball. So aim left with a slightly closed clubface at address

From a combined downhill and side slope(4) it is very difficult to play an accurate shot. Allow for the expected fade or slice and try to follow the slope with the clubhead at the start of the swing and through impact

How to play from poor lies

You will not get the ball out of a divot mark and flying with a straight-faced club. Resist the temptation to use any club more powerful than a 7-iron. Should the divot mark be quite deep, then consider taking a 9-iron or even a wedge. Always use a club with plenty of loft on it.

The correct position for the shot is to stand with the ball in the centre of the stance, or even back towards the right foot. This brings the hands in front of the clubhead which, in turn, promotes a steeper backswing than normal. You can then chop down on the ball and move it from the rut. It is less of a proper swing, more a stab shot, with little or no follow-through— if you like, squirting the ball out.

A lot of run can be expected as the ball will come out low if struck steeply and cleanly. Should the ball lie at rest at the start of the divot mark then you will have to take turf first.

Why no more than a 7-iron? Standing in front of the ball with the hands also in front reduces the loft on the clubface.

Tight for a bare lie

These should not really present a lot of problems but for the average-handicap golfer they do. When faced with a close lie a player freezes and mentally accepts that a poor shot from such a lie is inevitable.

This is negative thinking, but after putting the following instruction into practice you will be pleasantly surprised to find that a close lie will no longer be the hazard you have always recognized.

When playing from a close lie, steeper downswing is required to get the ball up and away, but do not consciously try to do this as there is a danger of exaggerating the movement.

All you need do is position yourself at address so that the ball is almost central in the stance with the hands slightly forward of the ball, and the clubface square to the intended line of flight. Automatically, this affects the backswing by making it more upright than normal from which a steeper downswing will result. At impact the ball will then be hit down, squeezing it between clubface and turf and driving it forward and up.

Naturally the ball will fly lower than is usual for the club being used, so allow for some run after landing. A more lofted club to compensate is the answer. However, to play a delicate pitch shot from a tight lie over a green-side bunker or some other obstacle, when the flagstick is near the hazard, is a difficult one. You need to bite into the turf so use a sharp-soled club such as a 9-iron. Unlike the longer shots from a similar lie, play the ball this time well *left* of centre. The feet and shoulders should be in an open position and the stance narrow. Hold the club down the grip somewhat for finer control with the clubface slightly open to the target line and the hands ahead of the ball.

As for the swing, it must be short, slow, deliberate and travelling along a track parallel to the feet line (out-to-in). Keeping the hands in front of the

To hit down steeply when playing from a divot mark, your hands should be well in front of the clubhead, the ball positioned off the right side

From a bare lie, to produce an upright backswing and steeper downswing, the ball should be central to the stance, clubface square to the target

 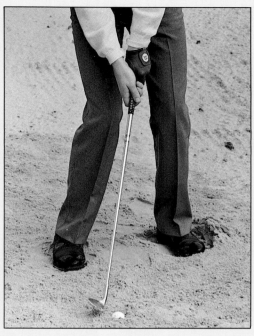 

For a short shot over an obstacle from a tight lie, use a sharp-soled lofted club. Open the face and stance, the ball off the left side

For a ball plugged in sand, adopt a slightly open stance, the ball just left of centre and the clubface square. Hit down and through

For a ball on the edge of a fairway bunker use a sharp-bladed club. Open the face and swing steeply down behind the ball

clubhead with little or no wrist action will offset any tendency that you may have to scoop the ball up and over the hazard. The loft on the clubface does that for you so do not quit on the shot.

Plugged in bunker

The only way to get the ball out is by taking plenty of sand, and to do that a firm grip is the first priority. Adopt a slightly open stance (left foot about one inch back from the right foot) and 'dig' the feet well in to get a firm footing. Have the ball positioned only a fraction left of centre.

The hands should be opposite the ball with the clubface square to target, but should the ball be deeply buried turn the clubface in a little so that it looks to be aiming a little left of the intended line. This will help neutralize the reverse turning of the clubhead on impact with the sand.

You will need to chop down into the sand close behind the ball and to achieve this the backswing must be on a much steeper plane than normal. It is not a traditional swing and some force has to be used. Swing the club a

little from out-to-in and parallel to the feet line keeping your hands in front of the clubhead throughout the action. It may be difficult but try hard to follow right through. Never leave the clubhead buried in the sand after making the stroke. You cannot expect to play a precision shot and it is reward enough to get the ball out.

Edge of bunker

You are close to the green and the ball has just tipped over into sand. There is a small ledge between the fairway and the ball, and you have one foot on the grass and the other in sand.

Use a sharp-bladed club, 9-iron or wedge, open the clubface and take an upright backswing. Hit steeply down into the turf at the side of the bunker and try to follow through if possible. It is a difficult shot and to get the ball on the green represents success.

Off a gravel path

Prepare to play a stiff-wristed shot from the middle of the stance, and feel that you are almost going to top the shot. In fact, what you do is try to

hit the ball with a flattish arc just below centre. Avoid hitting the ground – if only to save your club – and for the ordinary player the shot is a half-swing. You will have limited follow-through and the result should be a low flying shot with a lot of run.

Playing from the rough

First, some general advice for those of you who have problems playing these shots. The most common mistake is trying to make up distance after an initial error. Too many players succumb to temptation and risk a powerful club such as a 3-iron or 4-wood.

Unfortunately, escaping from the rough using one of the power clubs occasionally succeeds and the player having achieved it, say one time in thirty, remembers only that single success, forgets the twenty nine disasters, and stubbornly will not accept the inevitable.

Much better to accept the fact that you have probably lost a shot than to drop two or three attempting the near impossible. After all, having returned to the fairway it is still possible to get

How to play from poor lies

close to the pin with your third or fourth shot and have a chance of a single putt for par.

When in medium or deep rough it makes sense to get the ball back into play by the shortest route. Take, for example, the instance when you are in the rough and 190 yards from the green – a difficult shot at that distance even if you were on the fairway.

Your chances therefore from out of rough are virtually nil so forget your big clubs. When playing from the rough there is always a danger of the clubhead turning over (closing) at impact. It smothers the shot and the ball invariably flies low and to the left. The reason? As the club approaches impact the hosel and shaft get tangled up with the grass which turns the clubhead. To counteract this, address the ball with the clubface somewhat open and adopt a firm grip, especially with the left hand.

In addition, there is a cushioning effect of grass between the clubface and ball resulting in loss of control and reduced backspin. Such effects are very noticeable when playing from greenside rough. The smooth surface of the green is unable to hold the ball, whether it is high flying or low flying, and even tends to exaggerate the shot's runaway tendency.

If the rough is wet and the ball is lying quite well you have to guard against a 'flier' (a ball that flies further than it normally would for the same club and virtually out of control). This is caused by the wet grass coming in contact with the club first and producing a skidding effect – the wet grass between clubface and ball acting like grease. How to avoid a

Severiano Ballesteros plays a 'pop' shot from rough by the edge of the green

flier? A punch shot (which will not give sure control) is the only solution when the ball is in wet rough.

Semi-rough

This is the least of your problems and while a longish club may be possible you should always use a more lofted club than the one suitable from the fairway. Remember, the ball will run more when played from the rough.

Imagine a 5-iron fairway shot. The same ball in the rough would require a 7-iron, and with the extra run you are more than likely to finish with the same distance.

In wet conditions you need to guard against a 'flier' so position the ball midway in the stance with the

Graham Marsh lets the clubhead do the work on this shot from semi-rough

clubface square to the intended line. Take a three-quarter backswing and punch the ball forward. The follow-through will be shorter than usual for the same club. Expect quite a bit of run after the ball lands.

Should you be near the green in semi-rough, use a lofted club. Position yourself so that the ball is central in the stance and hold the club down the grip. Now, keeping your hands in front of the clubhead, play a sharp 'stab and stop' shot.

Medium-rough

It all depends this time whether the ball is lying down or sitting up. Both shots have to be treated with care. If the ball is right down in the roots of

Jack Nicklaus demonstrates his power as he recovers from thick rough

Tom Watson extricates himself from some of Royal Birkdale's savage rough during the 1983 Open Championship

the grass then the only solution is to take a very lofted club such as a 9-iron or a wedge. Adopt a slightly more open stance with the ball positioned towards the right foot. Use a more upright backswing and hit down on the ball. You have to accept some loss of distance.

When the ball is sitting up, it becomes possible to use a straighter-faced club, say, as much as a 4-iron. This time position the ball left side of centre in the stance as you will need to sweep the ball away. Take plenty of time over this shot and make sure that you do not go underneath the ball or it will be ballooned.

Deep-rough or fern
The only alternative you have here is whether you choose to use a wedge or a sand iron. Always reach for the heaviest club in the bag. Do not be greedy. Instead, settle for getting out of trouble even if it means playing out of the rough sideways.

Getting the ball back into play must be your first concern. Force the ball out rather than attempting a delicately judged stroke.

To get the best possible results when playing from such rough you will need to reduce the inevitable tangling of the clubhead and shaft with the long grass or tall fern during the backswing and downswing. To achieve this you must have the ball positioned right of centre after adopting an open stance. Take a steep backswing and strike the ball a descending blow with the hands ahead of the clubface. Naturally with this 'chopping' action there is little or even no follow-through.

Heather
When this type of growth has been cut short it is very misleading and often looks as if you can take a long club with confidence. However, this usually proves disastrous.

The ball looks to be sitting up beautifully but the 'branch stems' usually turn the clubhead right round and stop it dead. Utmost caution is necessary. Never go lower than a 5-iron even if the distance would seem to require a 3-wood. When in thick heather, play the shot as you would from deep-rough.

Thick clover
Should the ball be buried in this 'mushy' weed you will need to hit strongly through the shot and force the ball out. Use the same method as when playing from medium-rough.

At times you may find the ball lying in thin clover on the fairway where the mower has failed to cut because of some small ridge or undulation guarding the area. Do not be deceived by this seemingly fair lie. The reason? Invariably a ball hit out of clover will run after it lands because its soft stems and leaves have got between the clubface and the ball and reduced backspin. So always take one club less than you think you require to allow for the additional run.

Finally, before playing from any type of rough always take a note of which way the grass or stems are lying. When they are bent towards the target, address the ball well left of centre with the clubhead above ground – as you would in a bunker. This will help stop the rough interfering with the clubhead at the start of the backswing.

If the rough is lying away from the target – against the run of play – you must expect a lot of grass or similar, between the clubhead and ball at impact. This is unavoidable and not unlike when playing an explosion shot from sand when the clubhead does not make direct contact with the ball. Because of this cushioning effect between the clubface and ball, little distance and control can be expected.

In general terms, depending on the thickness of the rough, you will need to play this shot from the centre of the stance, use a steeper backswing and hit harder than usual. Experience here is the best teacher.

For all the poor lie shots there is one golden rule: whatever the circumstances the main object is to get the ball back into play.

Getting out of trouble

Even the greatest tournament players of our time all find trouble of some sort during virtually any round of golf. These, remember, are the experts with the luxury of being able to practise continually to eliminate any errors.

Now if they can get into trouble while knocking the ball round 6,800 yards, how much more likely will it be that you will stand with a furrowed brow looking down on one of the game's infuriating problem shots?

Thus we must all expect, either through a playing mistake or sheer bad luck, to experience these undesirable encounters of a close kind.

Winning, most decidedly, is more about being able to play the good recovery shot than it is about being fairly consistent around the course. If you can get yourself adequately back into play then you always have a chance of making par.

We all want to avoid trouble areas but if you will allow overwhelming caution to dominate then you will play every shot with a negative approach. Who dares wins! What we need is a balanced assessment of potential danger and the likelihood of golfing success.

Most club golfers leave the course trying to analyze the swing error that caused them to hit at least two or three of the bad shots that found trouble in their round – usually very conscious of how many shots they dropped through having to play from the difficult places.

The first piece of advice is not to analyze the reason for a particular bad shot, unless the error is a regular part of your game. Trouble is inevitable

With the ball in the centre of your stance, this brings your hands in front of the clubhead, which leads to a steeper backswing. Chop down on the ball with a punch-type shot with a three-quarter swing and the hands forward of the clubhead throughout with little follow-through

Always have a few practice swings to help get the feel. Stroke the putt and never give it a sharp tap on fast greens (illustration). With the blade at right angles to the chosen line, swing the putter low back and low through with a controlled stroke (photo)

and you will find it more profitable to learn to play the trouble shots with competence.

Ball in a divot mark

One of the most common problems is one that we all know and one that can be found even after a cracking shot. You walk up the fairway happily until you arrive to find the ball lying in a divot. Try to leave on one side the mental feeling that this is all so unfair. Whoever claimed that golf was a fair game, anyway? What you have to do now is to concentrate more on getting the ball out and flying towards the target.

You will not do that with a straight-faced club – and leave the woods in the bag. Do not be tempted to take any club more powerful than a 6-iron. If the divot mark is quite deep you may have to consider a 9-iron or even a wedge. Whatever your choice, always make sure that the club has an attractive amount of loft on it.

Loft is essential because the correct position at address is to have the ball in the centre of your stance, or possibly back towards the right foot. Automatically this brings the hands in front of the clubhead, and this leads to a steeper backswing than normal. You do not have to think about that because it is a completely natural response.

You can then chop it down at the back of the ball and move it from the rut. A punch-type shot, rather than a proper swing, is required. It is a three-quarter swing with the hands forward of the clubhead throughout. There is little or no follow-through.

Expect the shot to fly low and the

ball to run on after it lands. You will have struck steeply and cleanly, but when the ball rests at the far end of the divot mark (where the turf can almost form a step) you will need to hit down steeply and take earth before the ball. Hit the back of the ball first and then you can easily drive it into the 'step'.

A final word of explanation. Why draw the line at the 6-iron? It is because the hands are in front of the ball right through the action and this reduces the loft of the club.

Treacherous downhill putts

The next poser is how to finish close to the pin when faced with a treach-erous downhill putt. This is the most delicate of shots and, above all, requires feel: that is, feel of distance and clubhead movement.

Obviously you will study the part of the green involved carefully: the line, texture of grass, area immediately around the hole, and 'nap' or 'grain' (the direction in which the blades of grass grow), etc. This should give you some idea of what the ball will do as it loses momentum, and the strength needed to 'die' at the hole. Lee Trevino is a good example to follow. He always studies the putt from all angles, almost like an animal stalking its prey.

The best method in order to feel

Getting out of trouble

distance is to stroke a putt, but always have a few practice swings to help with this feel. *Never* give it a sharp tap on fast greens. You can usually control a stroking action but not the 'rap' method.

Try not to leave a fast downhill putt short. If it runs past the hole, then at least you will have given the hole a chance with the added advantage of an uphill putt back.

When faced with a short, curly two-foot putt, liable to borrow, make up your mind to be courageous and hit it firmly into the back of the hole. If it misses you are likely to be in trouble but practice will make perfect and your chances of sinking a firm putt are better than when trying to coddle it in. This is something that you will have to find out for yourself through experience.

On a long downhill slope, where the surface is like glass, it is best to trickle or finesse the ball towards the hole. Of course it is chancy and you will need a share of luck, no matter how nicely you play the shot. You can help your prospects by making sure that the putter blade is at right angles to the chosen line you wish the ball to follow and that you keep your head steady when stroking the putt. Never change your mind during the action, or rhythm is lost... and swing the putter low back and low through, near to the turf.

Ball plugged in a bunker

Headache number three is when the ball is well buried or plugged in a bunker. It could be a bunker full of wet sand, or it might be one containing soft, dry sand.

Dig your feet well into the sand (photo left). If the ball is well-buried, close the clubface slightly to offset the turning as the clubhead strikes the sand (illustration). Follow right through (photo right) and never leave the clubhead buried in the sand after the strike

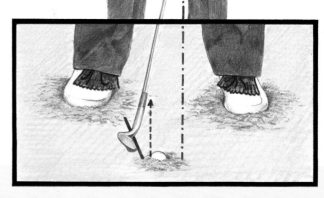

When you have to keep the ball low, a sharp stab shot with a 4-, 5- or 6-iron is needed. Direction is more important than length (illustration). Keep the hands in front of the clubhead at address and at all times through the shot (photo)

The advice is much the same for both circumstances except that in wet and firm sand it might be advisable to take a sharp-edged club such as a 9-iron to help cut through the sand. In normal conditions use the sand-iron, but the rest of the instruction is unchanged.

When a ball is buried you cannot get it out unless you take sand. To do that a firm grip is the priority. Adopt a slightly open stance with the left foot about an inch or so back from the right foot. Make sure you dig your feet well in to obtain a firm footing and in so doing you get an idea of the texture of the sand – this is important.

Remember that you are dealing with a buried or plugged ball, and the instruction will be somewhat different when the problem is that of the normal bunker shot.

Have the ball either in the centre of stance or a fraction right of centre. The hands should be ahead of the ball with the clubface square to target, but if the ball is fiendishly buried, close the clubface a little so that it seems to be aiming slightly left of the intended line. This closed face approach helps to dig the ball out and neutralize the turning of the clubhead on impact with the sand.

What you must do is chop down on the sand close behind the ball, and to achieve this make the backswing much more steep than is customary. It is a 'one-off' swing and some force has to be used. It may be difficult but try hard to follow right through, and never leave the clubhead buried in the sand after making the stroke.

Swing the club a little from out-to-in and parallel to the feet line, keep-ing your hands in front of the club-head during the action. It is impossible to play a precision shot but the reward is to get back on to grass.

Through the gap

Now to the problem of firing a shot through a narrow gap between trees or obstacles. What you must do is take your time and weigh up the situation carefully. If the gap is too narrow and the odds too heavily against, then a sideways or even backwards shot is the sensible course of action.

However, if you have decided that you have a reasonable chance of negotiating the gap, pick out the largest gap available rather than letting the direction of the hole dictate tactics. You know that the more lofted the club used, the quicker the ball will rise. It is much better if the shot stays low.

What is needed is a sharp stab shot with a 4-, 5- or 6-iron – naturally the height required governs the choice of club. Direction is more important than length. Take care that you are lined up correctly, clubface square to the intended line, and if it helps pick out a spot that you want the clubhead to travel over. The hands are ahead of the ball at address and throughout – this reduces clubface loft.

Because you are using a stiff stabbing action there is the danger of swaying in the same direction as the clubhead is travelling, which will cause the shot to be topped. To help eliminate this possibility, have a few practice swings before you actually play the shot.

When you meet the problem of playing out from under a bush or trees with branches brushing the ground, grip further down the shaft. You will have to settle, with a 4- or 5-iron, for a short stabbing action. Hold the club firmly and try to keep the hands leading the clubhead at all times during the shot.

The correct way to hook and slice

There are occasions during any round of golf when you may find yourself faced with a situation where you need to bend a shot round a tree or similar obstruction. Other times you may want to bend the shot away from a beckoning out-of-bounds area, or hold the ball against a strong crosswind. To be able to play such shots, at will, you must have the knowledge of how to hook and slice the ball.

Ask the club golfer how to play an intentional hook shot and the likelihood is that he will tell you to close the stance — that is, to have the left foot in advance of the right.

As far as stance is concerned that is not the way to hook the ball. The moment the player closes his stance he will automatically lock his left hip from turning out of the way in response to the clubhead as it nears impact. When this happens the clubhead will not have a free passage through the ball. The hands will arrive in front of the clubhead at impact and the probable result is a push shot out to the right of the target.

Better advice would have been to slightly 'toe-in' the clubface at address with the ball positioned towards right of centre in the stance and move the hands round somewhat to the right on the grip. How much you move the hands round will depend on the amount of hook requir-

To play a hook adopt a slightly open stance. Close the shoulders, position the ball right of centre in the stance, point the toe of the club inwards, and move the hands round to the right side of the club

The address position for achieving a hook will produce a flatter backswing and an exaggerated in-to-out swing path. Together with the shut clubface, this will start the ball out to the right. As the ball starts to lose momentum the side-spin imparted at impact will cause the ball to move to the left towards the end of its flight. Here a 6-iron is used to hit the ball a 4-iron distance

To play a slice adopt an open stance and shoulder position. Now position the ball towards the left foot, leave the clubface open at address, and move the hands to the left on the club and keep them in front of the clubhead throughout the swing action

The address position for achieving a slice will produce an upright backswing and an out-to-in swing path. The ball will start out to the left, but will gradually drift to the right. The clockwise spin causes the ball to lose distance, so here a 4-iron is being used

ed. Open the stance a few degrees and close the shoulders to the intended line of flight.

The altered grip coupled with the 'toed-in' clubface position at address will ensure a shut face at impact, while the closed shoulders and ball position help to flatten the backswing along a definite inside track. This, in turn, sets up an exaggerated swing path through the ball going from in-to-out.

As the clubhead comes into the hitting area the moderately open stance will allow the left hip to readily turn out of the way in response to the clubhead travelling through. The shot will start out to the right and then hook back into play due to the anti-clockwise spin imparted to the ball by the closed clubface at impact.

Make sure when playing for an intentional hook to select a less powerful club than one you would use for a normal shot for the same distance. The closed clubface delofts a club and turns, for example, the loft of a 6-iron into a 4-iron. Add to that the run on the ball that can be expected from a hooked shot.

The layman will tell you also that the correct way to play an intended fade or slice is just to open the stance (left foot back from the right). That may help to some degree, but more often than not a pulled shot straight to the left will result.

Keep the hands ahead

The best advice when a fade or slice is wanted is to open the clubface very slightly at address with the ball positioned opposite a point just inside the left heel. Then move the hands round a little to the left on the club; you can increase this grip alteration when a lot of slice is in demand. At the same time, open the stance and shoulders. Have the hands ahead of the ball, keeping them that way throughout the action.

This grip on the club keeps the clubface open throughout impact, helped by the hands being kept in front of the clubhead throughout the swing. The open stance and ball position, along with the shoulder line, will provide a more upright backswing giving a swing track from out-to-in across the line of flight, imparting spin on the ball. The shot will start out to the left with clockwise spin. When the forward thrust starts to weaken, the spin imparted at impact takes over and the ball curls to the right.

You will need to use a less-lofted club for the distance involved, because the open clubface together with the out-to-in swing track automatically weakens shot power.

Spend some of your practice time playing the intentional hook and slice. Then you will be prepared to play such shots that might be in demand when playing the course. Remember that a shot executed a number of times goes into the memory bank to be used when called upon.

How to combat the advancing years

The greatest strength of golf is the handicapping system whereby players of differing ability can compete with each other on equal terms. As you get older, you will find that you do not play quite as well as you did in your youth, but you *can* still enjoy the game to the full.

To know your limitations when playing golf is of the utmost importance irrespective of how well you play. The older you become, the more vital it is to come to terms with your deficiencies and to readjust your sights accordingly.

The long par four holes are usually the first holes where golfers may experience problems and it is no good thinking that what was, in the past, a drive and a medium iron can be reached with the same club twenty years later. Only vexation ensues if you adopt this misguided attitude.

As your body becomes less supple, it is all too easy to fall into incorrect swing habits. It is easy also to recognize these habits and take measures against them. Therefore, adjustments must be made when the body resists the complete pivot which is so essential for a proper swing. You still have to position the club correctly in the backswing so as to deliver the clubhead squarely into the back of the ball as always.

Since the ball is positioned to the side of you the swing path needs to be from the inside to straight through in order that the club should approach the ball on a shallow arc with the clubface squaring up at impact. This application will maximize distance whatever your clubhead speed. Few people understand that an out-to-in

When the body becomes less supple and pivoting is difficult, it is very easy to develop an out-to-in swing which gives you far too steep an angle of approach to the ball

swing is so damaging because of the steepish angle at which the club approaches the ball.

If, therefore, it is important to hit from the inside even when pivoting is more difficult, it is of real benefit to position the ball further back in the stance or more towards the right foot. This makes it easy to close the body position. There should be a conscious turning of the hips so that they face more behind the ball at address. This position also tends to strengthen the grip which means that both hands will be turned more over the shaft.

The awareness, at address, of the correct swing path into the ball should lead to much more of the effort coming from the hands and arms and much less from the body. At the same time, the change of grip will help deliver the clubface squarely.

The short game
The area of the game that does not require clubhead speed – the short game – should receive particular attention since it is in this department that shots can be made up and practice can be of real benefit. Much of our time and effort over the years has been spent hitting the ball a long way but once you recognize that huge distances are no longer attainable, the desire to practise the short game can often lead to some improvement in this very important department.

Certain adjustments in equipment can also be an advantage. The long irons with their lack of loft and poker-like feel do require good clubhead speed to be played succesfully. A 5-wood should, with its extra loft and greater feel, take the place of the 2-

and 3-irons. The driver should also have sufficient loft to put the ball in the air easily since the positioning of the ball further back in the stance will tend to de-loft the club. Lighter clubs are beneficial as we get older. Anything too heavy leads to the body taking over as opposed to the hands and arms applying the clubhead to the ball.

To make sure you bring the club into the ball from the inside a simple adjustment in your stance is necessary. Move the ball back towards your right foot and at the same time make a conscious effort to turn your hips so that they face behind the ball at address. This helps to strengthen your grip, making it easier to deliver the clubhead squarely

The point of practice

The handicapping system is one of golf's greatest features, as stated before, for it enables players of varying competence to enjoy a round together. The game is there to be played but if you wish to play better, practice is essential.

However, there is practice and practice. To simply hit as many balls as possible without thought and application will not do much other than to groove any mistakes that are already present in your game.

A competent professional, in a lesson, will diagnose mistakes and show how to eradicate them. He will prove his skill by getting the pupil, during the course of the lesson, to hit better shots. However, habit is a very difficult thing to overcome and the only permanent way is by correct and constant practice.

Clear concept essential

For those of you who enjoy practice and who are striving for improvement, a clear mental concept is essential before you start. It is equally important that the muscles are in a fit condition before the first balls are hit, otherwise the first few shots will not be good and the whole session will get off to a bad start.

Swinging a weighted club, or, more conveniently, taking two or three iron clubs together has two major benefits. It loosens the back muscles and helps to create the right tempo. Another appropriate exercise is to slip a club across the back with the arms behind the club. It is important, however, when doing this exercise, not to point each end of the club, when pivoting, to where the ball will be since that type of shoulder pivot would be far too steep. Take up the normal address position and pivot the shoulders, pointing the shaft at the ground some fifteen to twenty yards ahead of you.

Swinging any club normally, without a ball, should be repeated some ten to twenty times before the first ball is struck. Many players would claim to have a good practice swing but, of course, since there is no ball, there is no proof of the validity of this claim. The point is that without a ball, although the swing may look good, unless the clubface is square on impact, a shot with a ball will not be very effective. To practise swinging, pick some particular spot on the ground and endeavour to hit it. This spot, where the club reaches the bottom of its arc, should be varied, from the same stance, in order to create the necessary precision allied to the free-swinging motion is that easily achieved without a ball, since there is no element of fear.

Since the correct set-up, meaning clubhead, aim and body position, is so vital to good striking, it is essential to hit shots to a target. Lay two clubs on the ground, parallel to each other, so that the clubface and the foot alignment can be checked easily. It must be remembered that not only the feet need to be in position but, more importantly, the upper half of the body, too. The shoulders and hips should also be parallel to the line of aim.

By far the greatest proportion of golfers tend to slice the ball. This is

Sam Torrance practises under the watchful eye of his father, Bob

Swinging a weighted club, or, more conveniently, taking two or three iron clubs together has two major benefits. It loosens the back muscles and helps to create the right tempo. Another appropriate exercise is to slip a club across the back with the arm behind the club. It is important, however, when doing this exercise, not to point each end of the club when pivoting to where the ball will be since that type of shoulder pivot would be far too steep.

Take up the normal address position and pivot the shoulders, pointing the shaft at the ground some fifteen to twenty yards ahead of you

By far the greatest proportion of golfers tend to slice the ball. This is usually a result of overuse of the body with under-use of the hands and arms. The best practice for curing this type of mistake is to hit shots, especially using a 6-iron with feet together. From this narrow base, overuse of the body is immediately restricted

usually a result of over-use of the body with under-use of the hands and arms. The very best practice for this type of mistake is to hit shots with a 6-iron, with the feet together. From this narrow base, over-use of the body is immediately restricted, since an instant lack of balance will be felt. The thinking should be of the club being in the target direction at the top of the backswing, using your normal length of swing from where it is swung through the ball predominantly with the hands and arms.

From the inside

Do *not* practise full shots into a left-to-right wind. The position of the ball relative to the player means that the club should swing into the ball from the inside in order to release the club-face straight and square into the back of the ball. A left-to-right wind makes this movement very difficult to achieve, so even if this entails a considerable walk, hit balls against the wind or into a right-to-left wind. If you are working on your full swing, use a relatively easy club. A 6-iron is an easy club to use and yet needs a fairly full swing. Alternatively, use a no. 4-wood. For most, the long irons and driver should be avoided since they require a very good contact to produce any good shots. The whole essence of practice is to create new confidence, not to dissipate it.

One final word! Do not go on for too long when the exercise may well become boring. The mind loses its clarity of purpose and the muscles get tired eventually.

145

Practise your short game

Before outlining ways of practising the short game it is important to first point out that the ball will respond to the clubface as with all shots and that the clubface can be varied tremendously at impact. It can be in its normal position, square with the makers' loft, closed or open, strong, with the loft decreased, or weak when the loft has been increased. The great players vary the clubface position at impact through all the above dimensions to suit the shot required.

Under normal circumstances when you have short shots to play, you should first look at the ball to see what sort of lie you have, and then at the flag. You would then visualize how you want the ball to behave and select the club that would most easily give you the desired flight and roll. In many situations the execution of the shot would be kept as simple as possible, swinging the clubhead through the ball with the hands and arms letting the clubface do the job for which you have selected it.

What you require are means of developing feel since method without feel will avoid mishits but will rarely get the ball close to the hole – the main object of the exercise. The variants we have at our disposal, which determine how the ball will perform, are the clubface, the speed of the swing and the length of the swing.

To point out the two extremes, if you are playing a shot that is less than a full shot you can increase the loft of the club at address and make a full swing at much less than your normal speed. You will end up with a shot of less distance than the club would normally hit the ball but with the ball flying on a higher trajectory which flies slowly and lands very quietly. The other alternative would be to address the ball with the clubface loft somewhat decreased and using a

If you have difficulty in the short game with making good contact between club and ball follow this simple exercise. By placing a second ball a predetermined distance behind the one you intend to hit the desired angle of attack will be achieved. This second ball assists the address position by moving your weight more to the left side with your hands slightly ahead of the ball

If you are playing a less than full shot(1), by increasing the loft at address and making a full swing at less than normal speed, the ball will fly less distance than normal but on a higher trajectory. The ball flies slowly and lands softly. However, by decreasing the club loft(2) and using a much shorter swing plus the necessary speed for the distance required, the ball will take a lower flight and roll further on hitting the green

much shorter swing than normal, using the necessary amount of speed to propel the ball the desired distance. In this case you should produce a much lower flight and the ball would therefore tend to roll more on hitting the green.

With all these shots it is important, after having selected the club, to sense the length and speed of swing, and also the amounts of wrist, arm

Most golfers have no problems with playing chip and run shots, but when height is required there is a lack of confidence. A good practice aid for lofted pitch shots is to play to an upturned receptacle such as a bucket. Just increase the club loft and play the ball slightly more forwards with the hands opposite the clubhead. Do not concentrate too much on the method. Instead, try to visualize the flight of the ball

and body action that will produce the necessary shot. Pitching and chipping are a little more difficult than the standard shots since you have this added problem of how long to swing and how hard to hit. It is the development of these aspects that the short game requires and therefore practice becomes doubly important.

If you are someone who finds difficulty in actually making good contact with the club and ball, one of the best exercises is to position a second ball behind the one you are intending to strike. For the simple chip this should be twelve to fourteen inches behind since the angle of approach of the club is relatively shallow, but for the higher pitch shot this second ball should be positioned some seven to nine inches behind the ball. In each case the very presence of the second ball will assist the address position and move the weight on to the left side with the hands slightly ahead of the ball so that in the backswing the club will climb the necessary amount to give the desired angle of attack. This feeling should obviate the most common fault of scooping the shot whereby the bottom of the arc is arrived at behind the ball, resulting in either a fluffed or topped shot.

Spend time pitching shots into a receptacle. This can be anything from a bucket to an upturned umbrella, but it does have the considerable advantage of painting a picture of how the ball should fly. Most golfers can play the chip and run fairly easily, but immediately height is required there is a certain lack of confidence resulting in a quick *independent* flick of the club which can be disastrous.

Whenever you need more height on a shot the loft angle needs to be increased and therefore the ball will be played slightly more forward with the hands opposite the clubhead. For extreme height the clubface would also be open and the swing path out-to-in. To compete with a friend or friends is quite the best practice since to some extent it takes the mind off the method and aims it more at visualizing the flight of the ball which is so desirable.

Another good exercise, again to be indulged in in a competitive way, would be to pick a spot a certain distance from the flag (between forty and 120 yards) and play shots from the same distance with various clubs. This helps enormously to gain an appreciation of how the clubface can be varied along with the speed and length of the swing to give the desired result. Past generations were rather better at what is suggested than the modern player who automatically takes a wedge for all these shots and never quite develops the right feel. Severiano Ballesteros comes to mind immediately as someone who learnt his fantastic short game by practice and making one club hit all sorts of different shots.

Lots of fun, and also of great benefit, is to compete from different places and distances with the same club, as opposed to the same distance with varying clubs. The lies and degrees of difficulty should all vary, again to develop feel. When playing, obviously you use the club that will do the job most easily, but if feel has been developed by the above suggestion the results will be much improved.

Soft shots
Along with modern architecture, and this applies particularly in the United States, most greens are elevated to some extent, to help with the drainage and overall construction of the greens. This means that many of the short shots are played to an elevated green and thus the ball pitches on the green flying at a much lower effective trajectory than if the green was at the same height as the player. It becomes doubly important therefore to be able to hit 'soft' shots, whereby at impact the loft of the club has been increased. Most players tend to de-loft the lofted clubs too much at address for these high shots, and either mishit the shot by trying to put on extra height in the hitting area or they will settle for going beyond the flag. Pitching balls to an elevated target should also become part of the exercise and also playing shots to a green set below.

In this latter situation the ball will strike the green at an increased trajectory and will usually finish some distance short of the hole.

All of the above is most beneficial and if practice can be done with like-minded friends, not only is it most helpful but it is also tremendous fun.

Chapter 7 THE MIND GAME

During a three-hour round of golf, you will spend only two or three minutes actually striking the ball. The remaining time, therefore, leaves your mind open to all kinds of distractions, mental pressures and negative thoughts. Training your mind to work for you rather than against you on the golf course is a major factor in improving your game. Concentration is not something that can be produced at will, but this chapter can help you to guide your thought processes in the right direction, show you how to banish any negative thoughts and lower your scores, how to learn from your mistakes, how to improve through imitation and instruct you on what tactics to use for matchplay.

Golf is played in the mind, too

Nobody is quite sure whether a vivid imagination is a boon or a burden for the golfer. Certainly an imagination that can be kept firmly under control can be a great advantage. It allows you to adapt your own technique by copying others; it enables you to visualize the flight of each shot before striking the ball; and to rehearse mentally what you are trying to do. However, an imagination that is not kept firmly under control can be one of the worst psychological problems to counter.

Frequently the club golfer is hampered by an imagination that runs wild. Take the example of players approaching a little pitch shot over a bunker. Frequently they are faced with a shot they do not like; begin to think of how many under or over par they are; of what will happen if the ball dribbles into the bunker; visualize themselves being in the bunker and then not being able to get out; think of what an idiot they will look to the people watching; worry about the ball shooting across the green into the clubhouse window, and so on and so forth.

This is something that is far too common for comfort. The same thing can happen, of course, with the professional golfer. It is all too easy to find yourself standing on the eighteenth tee needing a four for a sixty nine, imagining the cheque you are likely to receive if you produce it, going to the other extreme and imagining the ball slicing away into the bunker you want to avoid, becoming nervous of the people watching you, and all manner of other fairly destructive thoughts arise.

Playing golf well requires just the right amount of thought and imagination. It requires sufficient thought to assess the situation properly and enough imagination to help execute the shot well. On the other hand, it requires that the brain is kept sufficiently free and empty of thought to avoid being negative and hence destructive.

What you need to be able to do is to control the mental situation under which you are playing very firmly. If you have a vivid imagination then there are several ways in which you can make this work for you. For example, if there is a tee shot on your own particular course where you always feel happy and your thoughts are positive, then try to imagine yourself standing on that particular tee over and over again. Rehearse the feeling of setting up to that particular drive and try to be able to repeat this mental situation whenever you find

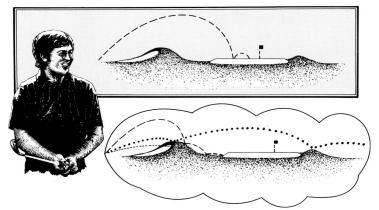

The attitude of the professional to a tricky shot is often completely different to that of the club golfer. The professional will mentally rehearse his swing, visualize the spot where he wants the ball to land, and imagine the flight of the ball landing on his chosen target. The club player, however, may imagine the ball dribbling into a bunker and then perhaps being unable to get out of it, or instead, see his ball shooting across the green into trouble on the other side

yourself on a strange course and on a tee that is not particularly endearing. Mentally whisk yourself back to that tee shot at home that always makes you feel comfortable.

After all, any drive is simply a question of you standing on the square yard or so of ground with a ball on a peg and trying to blast it away down the fairway. Similarly, if you are faced with a drive out over a lake and you are a long-handicap golfer who does not like the prospect of this shot, then control the mental situation, mentally make the lake disappear, imagine yourself on a driving range or whatever, and forget what is ahead of you. Learn to ignore the out-of-bounds fences and the people watching, the bunker that is encroaching on your driving area, and so on.

Develop a routine

This is largely a question of developing a perfect ritual to each shot, setting yourself up and thinking very positively about yourself, the ball, the ground you are standing on and so on, while ignoring as far as possible what is out ahead of you. Mental practice can do a great deal of good in this way. If you hit balls fairly frequently on a practice ground, then spend a few minutes a day imagining yourself standing on the practice ground, firing balls at your target. Build up the mental image of performing these shots. Soon you should find that you can take this picture out on to the golf course with you. You should be able to stand in the middle of any fairway, facing a shot to the green and yet have the same positive mental picture you had on the practice ground.

Try to appreciate that all golf shots are simply a matter of you standing on your square of ground with the ball in front of you, the idea of each shot simply being to strike that ball as accurately as possible to the flag. If you can control the mental situation, then the approach can remain consistent regardless of what obstacles or hazards lie ahead of you.

In a similar way, you should be able

When you find yourself confronted by a difficult tee shot, imagine that you are on a tee at your home course where your thoughts are positive and you feel confident of hitting a good shot. Instead of worrying about the hazards facing you, pretend you are on that favourite tee at home. Any drive is simply a question of standing on a square yard of ground with the ball on a tee-peg, and trying to hit it down the fairway

to control your mental approach to scoring. All too easily players become demoralized if they are several over par or losing a match, or become nervous if they are under par or in sight of winning. What you need to do is to try to decide on the mental approach that brings out the best in your game of golf.

Do you do your very best if you tell yourself that every shot is to win the Open tournament? On the other hand, are you the sort of player who plays in the Open and yet does his best while playing a few holes exercising the dog! You need to decide just what sort of player you are and then put yourself in that position.

If you are a player like Tony Jacklin or Seve Ballesteros, then you will probably perform your best when the adrenalin is flowing fast and furiously and you are telling yourself that every putt is for a million dollars. Then again, if you are like Ben Hogan or Neil Coles, or indeed the majority of professional golfers, then you are probably best playing with a fairly ice-cool approach – if anything, you should try to play down the importance of the occasion.

Do not assume necessarily that you are the first kind of player when in reality you always crack at the last minute under pressure. Learn which situation you respond to best and then mentally try to control that situation. If appropriate, pretend that the game does not matter, pretend you do not really care whether you win, convince yourself that it is just another round on a Sunday morning.

The physical game of golf is simply a question of hitting the ball from a spot on the ground in front of you to a target so many yards away. The difficulties you encounter are largely ones of your own making, produced by the fact that your imagination is being at its most destructive.

Improve through imitation

Children have a great capacity for imitation and, for this reason, are able to learn physical skills comparatively easily. They have no real fear about acquiring new skills, have few of the inhibitions that adults have about failing, and will take on each new challenge with enthusiasm. Words mean relatively little to children up to perhaps twelve years of age, and the acquirement of new physical skills can be imparted usually by adult example.

By contrast, most adults try to learn from words and explanation. Most forms of education gradually teach us to think in the abstract with words as our main learning tool. Imitation tends to be pushed to one side and for most adults is used only subconsciously. When adults start to learn new physical skills like golf, what they need to do is to assess their own attitude towards learning and adopt a more childlike approach. If the adult can take himself back to learning like an eight- or nine-year-old then there is a much greater chance of success. Adults need to realize that imitation can still be the major and most useful route to learning. Yet, what most people do is over-analyze everything they see in golf, trying to explain it to themselves in words rather than looking simply at an example in front of them and copying it.

An adult and a child both looking at a professional golfer and trying to learn from him would assess his movements in two entirely different ways. The child would simply look at the example, create a mental picture and imitate it quite successfully. The adult, by contrast, would probably

The rhythmic tempo of Nick Faldo's swing is one which all golfers should try and imitate

use words to describe what the professional was doing, try to translate those words into instructions to the body and then produce what is thought necessary. The actual picture created is probably neither consciously nor subconsciously used.

Yet adults can learn most certainly by imitation when and if they put their minds to it. Many golfers will quite openly say that their own golf improves after watching professional golf on television. This is because the golfer has a picture of the correct

action presented on the screen for several hours, and therefore some kind of an after-image is retained. Although golfers will say that this is what happens, however, they often do not look actively for an example in their own learning.

Unfortunately, golf teaching tends not to produce sufficient examples. It is easy for a professional to stand aside and instruct pupils in what he wants them to do. The professional takes a relatively passive role in the lesson. In sports such as tennis or squash, the professional is providing a constant example of what to do. The golf professional should do likewise and spend more time demonstrating to the pupil what is required of him. Of course, pupils think that they are not getting their money's worth unless they are hitting the golf ball continually. They do not want to spend most of the lesson watching the professional hitting shots and having only the odd go at imitating. Pupils gradually mould the professional into teaching in the way in which they want to be taught. They want explanation as well as theory, and usually an excess of it.

If you are having problems with your long game, your swing or any of the short game techniques, look for an example on television or from your own club professional, and try and slot yourself into that picture with the minimum amount of linguistic interpretation and instruction. Learn to learn as children do; after all, they are the experts at acquiring new physical skills through their use of pictures and imitation, and you *can* do exactly the same.

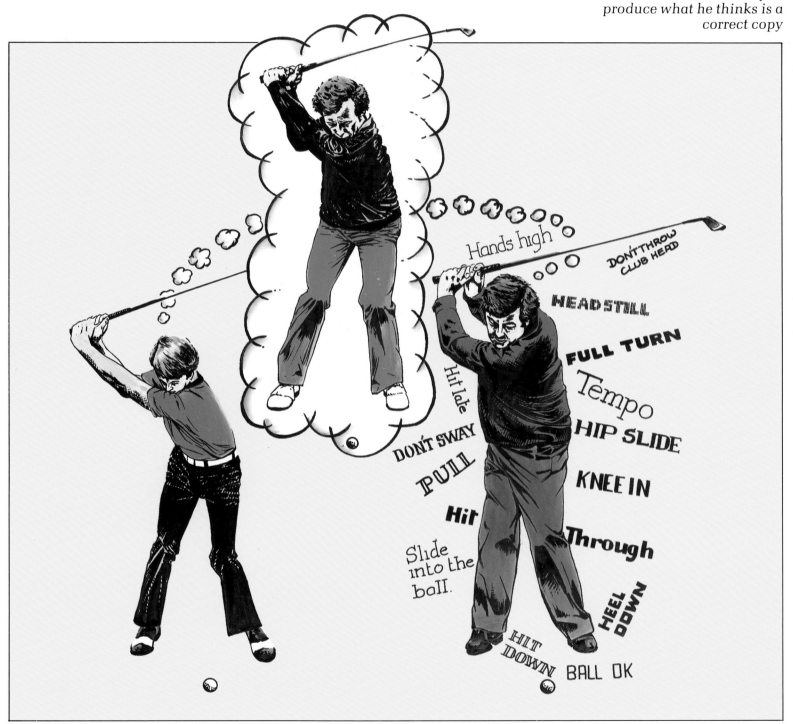

151

What you can learn from playing badly

Many years ago, G.K. Chesterton coined the phrase: "If a thing is worth doing well it's worth doing badly." Golf indeed is such a great game that it is not only those who play to a professional standard who find it enjoyable. There are many hundreds of thousands of golfers who play the game badly and yet still find it fascinating and absorbing. Many of them have no real hope of improving but clearly go on enjoying the sport without any real yearning to improve.

In fact, you often hear the low handicapper or professional showing amazement at why some long-handicap players bother to play the game at all. And yet, in reality, the long-handicap player and particularly the real no-hoper, has a real lesson to teach those of us who aspire to play the game properly and to a high standard, for they have learnt the art of playing bad golf.

Learning to fail

Playing golf badly is far more difficult in many ways than playing golf well. Learning to fail, to play badly and to be seen to play badly, takes far more guts and courage than performing like a champion. In many ways learning to hit and accept thoroughly bad golf shots and to play some ridiculously bad rounds of golf are at the heart of learning to improve. Many a good golfer never learns to accept his or her own shortcomings and failings. As a result there is always a weakness in the game. The no-hoper, by contrast, often masters perfectly acceptance of his own failings. He has no choice!

In order to be a champion at any sport you must have high standards and a perfectionist attitude. Without this there is always a limitation in the desire to improve. However, combined with the total dedication and perfectionist attitude of the champion has to be an acceptance of the inevitable failures at golf.

Golf is not a game like many others where the top-class player can virtually become unbeatable throughout one or more sporting seasons. In golf this just does not happen. However good the player may become, his performance will fluctuate more from day to day than in almost any other sport. A top player can shoot sixty three on one day and seventy eight on the next without really knowing why and without any really noticeable change in the play of each shot.

In order to improve at golf it is

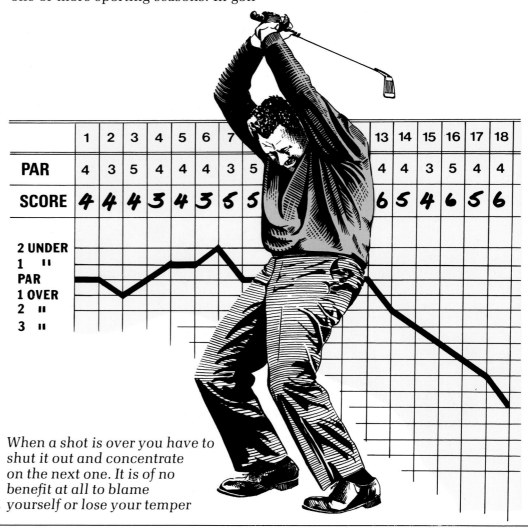

When a shot is over you have to shut it out and concentrate on the next one. It is of no benefit at all to blame yourself or lose your temper

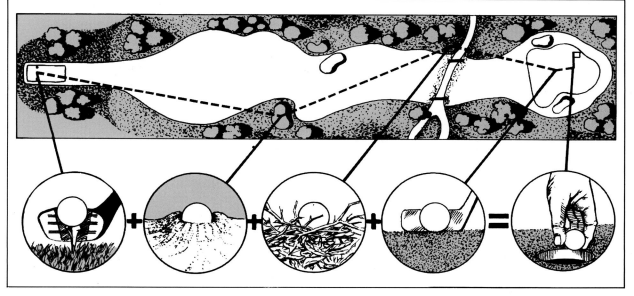

Each shot demands your full attention. You must ignore what has gone before and not worry about the shots that are still to come. Each shot is a separate task to be performed as well as possible

necessary to be able to cast aside bad shots and not to allow these to affect the next shot to be played. Each shot is a separate task to be performed as well as possible. It is necessary in playing each shot to isolate that specific task and to cast aside frustration and worries over shots that have gone before or, indeed, those that are still to come.

In particular, the player who strives hard for improvement and success often becomes over-critical of any shot that is noticeably less than perfect. And yet the perfect golf shots happen rarely in any round of golf. At any level there are going to be bad shots and even a few extremely bad or disastrous shots. It is impossible to play the game without these figuring in almost every round and certainly in every tournament.

It is vital to learn to detach yourself from every shot once that particular shot is over and done with and to concentrate on the next one to hand. Bad shots must be cast aside and forgotten or at least accepted until the game is over and you can then review the whole round with a critical eye without affecting what is to come. All too often, players will hit a poor shot, chastize themselves for the error, inwardly punish themselves all the way to the next shot, perform badly as a result of inner anguish with this

shot and then gradually deteriorate throughout the whole round. The art of playing good golf requires the ability to focus the mind entirely on the present and the near future without ever looking back at bad shots that have gone before. By all means, they can be reviewed very briefly in order to uncover some likely technical error, but each shot, having gone, is a thing of the past.

A tremendous desire to reduce any errors is still essential, of course, to playing good golf. However, acceptance of such errors is almost more important to many people. Golf is virtually a unique game. It is one of the few games where each player plays a ball from the start to the finish of the game without that ball being influenced in any way by another person. In most ball games, players share a ball. This means that in most sports any shot facing you is influenced by other people. Your return of service at tennis, for example, is dependent upon the strength of service of your opponent.

No excuses in golf
In many ways this gives you an excuse. Your opponent may have played well rather than you playing badly and any shot missed can be put down to his excellence of performance to a certain extent.

In golf there are no excuses. Everything that happens to your golf ball is your doing. Except with some most unlikely disaster – a rub of the green – the position of every single shot you play on the golf course is your responsibility, whether played there, teed there or dropped there. There is no-one else you can blame for your failure in matchplay by kidding yourself that your opponent was many under par in beating you, or you may find comfort in playing foursomes with a partner to lean on. Ultimately, however, each shot is your responsibility.

Why indeed do many club players find stroke-play so much more difficult than matchplay? It only involves playing a number of golf shots to the best of your ability and writing down the number you take for each hole. The true difference is that at the end of the round there is a score card that you and your marker have to sign telling everyone the truth about how you played. The card does not lie and you have to accept responsibility for what it says.

Vital to playing golf well is to be able to accept failure while still being a dedicated perfectionist. Realizing the inevitability of bad shots and bad scores on the golf course in the way in which the golfing rabbit does may set you on the right road to success.

Banish negative thoughts and lower your scores

There are three distinct stages in learning to become a good golfer. The first stage is to learn to swing the club in a reasonably smooth and technically correct way. The second stage is one of learning to swing the club with exactly the same technique once you have the ball on the ground in front of you. The third stage is to be able to take that same swing out onto the golf course and make it stand up to all forms of competitive pressure.

Sad to say, many golfers never really master even the first stage. Very often the reason for this is that they are so intent on getting the ball round the golf course with the least possible pain and suffering that they do not give themselves sufficient time and practice to develop the correct swing.

However, having developed a good swing without the ball, the next stage is to learn exactly the same thing with the ball. This requires a certain degree of patience – both from the professional and the pupil – and sufficient practice at striking the ball so that you produce the correct kind of contact. Many golfers reach the stage where they can swing the club in a fairly orthodox manner and so produce reasonably good results on the practice ground, but then find it almost impossible to strike the ball as well once they venture out onto the golf course. Frequently this kind of player becomes frustrated by the game because no amount of lessons on a practice ground seems to produce improved results on the golf course.

One of the problems here is that the situation in which you find yourself on the golf course varies constantly and no amount of professional coaching on a practice ground can possibly cover all the different shots you are likely to be faced with. However, the most basic problem for the kind of golfer who is an under-achiever on a golf course is that he or she simply does not think correctly when playing as opposed to practising.

On the driving range, you may well be faced wih a wide open space and simply a target to hit at. There is no particular pressure on you if you miss the target and your mind is either likely to be concentrated on the technique that you are trying to develop or is going to be focused on the flag at which you are aiming. Once you get out onto the golf course there are all kinds of distractions and also extra difficulties to master.

One of the best ways of improving a player's ability round the golf course is to get the pupil to think out loud so that he or she relates exactly what is going on in his or her mind prior to striking the ball. Most people are slightly inhibited about doing this at first and require prompting. It soon becomes apparent, however, that many of their thoughts are totally destructive as far as playing round the course is concerned. Players will often stand on a tee, look down the fairway and then think to themselves, "Whatever I do, I must not slice into those trees". Alternatively, they may say, "Please do not let me hook the ball out of bounds". What they are doing is falling into the great trap of giving themselves a set of negative commandments.

Visualize your shots

The whole philosophy in teaching is to tell the pupil *what* to do and never what *not* to do. The reason is this: if you give yourself some kind of instruction where a physical movement like the golf swing is concerned, you should also be giving yourself an image – either a visual image or an image of the movement required.

In no way can you visualize something that is negative. If therefore, you say to yourself, "What I must not do is to slice the ball", the visual image that you have in your brain is that of a slice. In other words, you are going to visualize exactly the same thing whether you are telling yourself to slice or not to slice. What happens, in fact, is that the image that you are conjuring up of the slice – the very thing you do not want to produce – acts as a form of instruction to your mind and muscles and encourages the wretched slice you did not want in the first place.

To a certain extent, this kind of imagery is more important for the low handicapper and the top-class golfer. Most top-class golfers will only produce a really bad shot on the golf course if they cannot get the right picture of the shot they are trying to produce. Under competitive pressure your ability to produce the right kind of picture sometimes tends to be inhibited and the golfer may find it almost impossible to cut out images of the shots that are the danger points he wants to avoid.

The top-class golfer can respond rather more to the instructions he gives himself and can virtually hook or slice the ball at will, without making any really noticeable changes of technique, simply by thinking of the way in which he wants to bend the ball. If all the images remain positive then this can work for him, but if he allows the wrong kind of thought to creep into his mind, a negative thought often acts as his instruction to produce the very shot he did not want.

For the club golfer it is still vital, however, to produce the right kind of *positive* image of the shot you want to produce. If you find yourself standing behind a bunker faced with a little shot over it and onto the green, you must have an image in your mind of the type of action you are trying to produce in the swing and also how the ball should fly. It is no use standing behind the bunker and imagining the ball dribbling along the ground. If you imagine this, then you are giving yourself the wrong set of instructions and your muscle memory will do its best to trickle the ball into the sand!

Exactly the same thing can happen with a short putt. If you imagine the ball being dragged away to the left, you will drag it away to the left. If, on the other hand, you can train yourself to think of the ball diving into the hole, then you have every chance of sinking the putt.

The way in which you think about a shot before you produce it acts as a kind of dress rehearsal for what is to follow. Try to imagine the way in which your arms and legs are going to move in the swing, the feeling of the contact with the ball and – most important – the way in which the ball is going to fly. This split-second preparation before every shot is tuning your body to produce the required movements.

The 12th hole at Augusta National, site of the United States Masters, is no place for negative thoughts

There is also another lesson in this for every golfer. If you are having some kind of problem with one or two particular shots on the golf course, such as a tee shot that you do not like, it is well worthwhile spending a few minutes just sitting and imagining yourself doing the shots correctly. If you think of that nasty difficult short hole and imagine yourself landing the ball on the green over and over again, with a smooth swing and controlled balance, then you have every chance of producing exactly the same set of mental instructions and the same swing when you return to the golf course the next day.

If, on the other hand, when you set up to the tee shot all you can imagine is the disastrous efforts you have made there recently, the odds are that you will produce exactly the same failure once more. This strengthens the wrong pattern and the wrong thoughts and the shot gets worse.

Remember, then, that all your thoughts in the golf swing must be positive. You must not imagine something negative because imagining what you do not want only acts as an instruction to your body to produce just this. Use the two or three seconds before hitting the golf ball as your mental dress rehearsal and never think in terms of the shot that you are trying to avoid.

Matchplay tactics that can work for you

Most club golfers find stroke-play a far more demanding test of golf than matchplay. In stroke-play the score has to be written down and there is no way of covering up — the score is there on the card and everyone knows how well or badly a golfer has played. In matchplay it is easy to assume that a score is better than it is, in fact, and for this reason, matchplay is psychologically less demanding than stroke-play. However, matchplay does exert its own psychological pressures which may arise at various stages during a match, and learning how to cope with these and relate them to your own position can help you win more matches.

Top-class players have distinctly different views on how to approach matchplay. Many players will say that you should try simply to play each shot to the best of your ability and build up a score as you would in stroke-play. If you can build an excellent medal score, better than your opponent's, then a win should follow. The whole idea of this approach to the game is that you are affected as little as possible by what your golfing opponent is doing.

The less common approach to matchplay golf is that you adjust your style to react to what your opponent does. However, it is not at all safe to make assumptions about your opponent's shots. You can be in a perfect position while your opponent is in difficulties and if he then plays a devastating shot from the rough, your assumption of a win can quickly be changed into an actual loss

The other approach to matchplay — perhaps the less commonly adopted one — is that you definitely view what your opponent is doing and play a cat-and-mouse game against him, adjusting your play accordingly. The difficulty with this approach is that it is easy to make the wrong predictions as to what your opponent is likely to do. There are too many unknown quantities in golf so it is not safe to assume anything at all about your opponent's shots. It is easy to find yourself in a position where your opponent is in trouble so you play safely because of this and then your opponent hits a devastating shot from the rough and holes the putt for a birdie. You, by contrast, assumed that a win was in the bag, played safely and lost the hole.

It is better to try and adopt the former approach and to make a good score. This way you do not fall into the trap of making a wrong prediction about your opponent's performance — you simply ignore his shots as much as possible, concentrate on hitting each shot you play to the best of your ability, play each hole in the lowest possible score, and wait and see what happens. Obviously there has to be an element of being slightly more aggressive with the odd chip or putt if you know that it has to go in for a half but such alteration of your own approach should take place only once your opponent's ball is in the hole and you know his score.

Even on the green it is so easy to assume that your opponent will hole a putt of five feet for a par and so you attack the hole too boldly with your long putt for a par, run it four feet

past, he misses his and you miss yours and lose the hole. Added to this, you suffer mental irritation and despondency; whereas he gets a tremendous boost at his good fortune. So, do not predict what is likely to happen — only adjust your own game when you are absolutely certain what you have to beat or equal.

One of the great arts of matchplay, as indeed with stroke-play, is to keep your mind firmly in the present, never allowing yourself to look back and regret failures nor to look forward and worry about what is likely to happen in the future. The art of keeping the brain thinking firmly of only the shot in hand is one that is central to good scoring in golf. It is all too easy to succumb to regretting what has gone before, particularly if a big lead is beginning to slip away, and in this case it is even more essential to stay in the present. It is also important to remember that in matchplay, huge changes in fortune can take place. One player can win six holes on the

first nine and be six up; the other player can just as easily win six or seven on the second nine. For this reason, you should never feel any sympathy whatever for your golfing opponent just because you have a sizeable lead.

The last mental trick about matchplay is always to assume that your opponent will hit the perfect shot. If he is about to hit a chip towards the hole, then assume he will hole it. Train yourself to imagine him producing the perfect shot. If he then fails, you receive a psychological boost. If, however, he succeeds, then it comes as no surprise and you are not psychologically wounded because that is all you expected. If you can adopt this mental outlook, then every less-than-perfect shot by your opponent will give you a boost, and the odd perfect shot will not unnerve you. Train yourself to attack the course, to ignore your opponent as far as possible and to play relentlessly until victory is secured.

INDEX

Numerals in *italics* refer to illustrations

Acknowledgements

Photographs
We would like to thank the following for supplying photographic material for use in the book:

Ken Adwick: pages 104, 105, 113, 136, 137, 138 and 139
Peter Dazeley: front cover (main picture and centre right) and pages 9 (bottom right), 12, 19, 23, 24-25, 30-31, 32, 33, 45, 61 and 76
Lawrence Levy: pages 7, 34 and 35
Jonathan Roan: page 9 (main picture)
Phil Sheldon: front cover (top and bottom right) and back cover and pages 11, 13, 15, 28-29, 37, 38, 43, 50, 59, 63, 67, 74, 75, 77, 78, 79, 84, 87, 89, 90, 91, 92, 110, 114, 115, 118, 121, 128, 129, 131, 132, 133, 134, 135, 140, 141, 144, 150 and 155
Stephen Szurlej: pages 26-27

Illustrations
The illustrations throughout the book and on the back cover are by Ken Lewis and have been supplied by *Golf World* Magazine.